Endorsements

A story-filled, biblically-informed, reader-friendly book that proposes a profoundly simple way to practice peace: good guestwork! Wisdom fills the pages of this book. I recommend it to all who desire to be peacemakers in our troubled world.

—Al Tizon, PhD, affiliate associate professor of missional and global leadership, North Park Theological Seminary

This book is a timely and prophetic invitation to follow Jesus where he is most often found—at the margins. A refreshing and courageous contribution to missiology and interfaith engagement.

—John Azumah, PhD, executive director, The Sanneh Institute

A must-read... Packed with personal vignettes and remarkable missiological insights which beg for sustained group discussion. This volume would make excellent Sunday School or book study curriculum.

—Dorothy Jean Weaver, professor emerita, Eastern Mennonite Seminary

A complete re-imagination of the role of missions in an easy-to-read, relatable form. A must read for anyone seeking to engage their neighbors near and far.

—Jonathan Rudy, Peacebuilding Global

You need this book in your library.... deeply respectful and insightful reflection on hospitality and peace—not merely as social courtesy, but as a spiritual imperative shared across both faiths.

—Joseph Kwoma Ngolla, Eastleigh Fellowship Centre, Mennonite Church Kenya

I have seldom read such a powerful and prophetic invitation to live joyfully and fearlessly as strangers, as followers of Jesus, in our polarized world.

—Linford Stutzman, professor emeritus, Eastern Mennonite University

A seminal work for understanding interfaith dynamics, and also necessary reading for anyone who longs to live as a disciple of Jesus in a global way.

—Regina Hassanally, bishop, Evangelical Lutheran Church in America

Challenging and inspirational, even prophetic. There are sentences that will cause the reader to stop and wrestle with Scripture and the Lord about what they've just read. The stories within are parables that upend many of our common assumptions and theological excuses. I recommend it for all who seek to follow Jesus faithfully as both guests and hosts.

—Lorri Bentch, mission team director, Eastern Mennonite Missions

A powerful plea. Defies easy categorization...vivid and moving stories of surprising encounters.

—Anicka Fast, visiting researcher, Boston University Center for Global Christianity and Mission

Sensenig's masterpiece underscores the significance of living as followers of Jesus at the margins. The personal stories here highlight love's power to heal divides. Highly recommended.

—Nelson Okanya, leadership consultant; former president, Eastern Mennonite Missions

What a timely book! Not simply a feel-good exhortation to be nice to the other—it is challenging and enlightening constructive theology. While readable, accessible, and engaging, this book offers a deep and transformative vision for embodying the way of Jesus in thought and practice.

—Ted Grimsrud, senior professor of peace theology, Eastern Mennonite University

A rare combination of brilliance, depth, and lived experience... Theology with a beautiful rhythm of reflection and practice.

—Eduardo Lara Reyes, MDiv, pastor

Winsomely shows that mission that takes on the stance of a guest may be messy, but that in that messiness we encounter the God who welcomes all people as Host.

—Alain Epp Weaver, author of *Service and the Ministry of Reconciliation*

We need strangers. We need difference. We need bridges. We need to be—not just hosts—but guests. Tells of honor, rejection, service, and fear... A timely and countercultural message for the global church.

—Debbi DiGennaro, author and educator

Can a book be both a page-turner and one that demands slow re-reading and reflection? *Good Guestwork* is that kind of book!

—Dr. Mike Medley, professor emeritus, Eastern Mennonite University; former Presbyterian mission worker in Pakistan

This book represents the kind of moral imagination that sees peace as a creative art.

—Nik Bredholt, secretary general, Religion & Society, Denmark

A call to embody Jesus in the presence of others. As a Christian, I need others; I need to learn from Muslims, and vice versa. This book calls to mind the concept of *ubuntu*: I am because we are.

—Siaka Traoré, pastor, Église Mennonite du Burkina Faso

Dares the church to reject fear and rivalry and instead embrace the costly way of hospitality with our Muslim neighbors... A prophetic call to recover the gospel of peace, to risk friendship, and to discover Christ on the other side of our comfort.
—J. Matthew Barnes, PhD, vice president, Asbury Theological Seminary

Eminently readable, personal, vulnerable stories that summon followers of Jesus back to our ancient calling—to love God and our neighbors, even across differences.
—Jon W. Carlson, pastor, Forest Hills Mennonite Church

This remarkable book combines memoire, theology, ethics, and social psychology... A prophetic call for honest, dynamic mutual persuasion.
—Charles Randall Paul, founder and president, Foundation for Religious Diplomacy

For those hungry for specific models of faithfulness in tumultuous times... Read this work in study groups, for personal devotions, and for a path toward conversation across difference.
—Nancy R. Heisey, professor emerita of biblical studies, Eastern Mennonite University; former president, Mennonite World Conference

A strong call to churches in the Western world (and elsewhere) to reexamine their identity and practices in order to embody the ministry of reconciliation.
—Neal Blough, professor emeritus, Faculté Libre de Théologie Evangélique, Vaux-sur-Seine, France

I am deeply grateful for this book. With stories, biblical wisdom, and a heart for reconciliation, it will encourage any follower of Jesus who longs to live out the gospel of peace in everyday life.
—Aldo Siahaan, pastor, Philadelphia Praise Center

This book will transform the way you think about mission, evangelism and Christian-Muslim relations.
—Daniel Nygaard Madsen, international director, Center for Church-Based Development, Denmark

Inspiration and encouragement for those investing in interfaith dialogue and bridge-building... A ground-level credible window into reconciliation.
—Dave Osborne, retired educator, relief and development worker in the Middle East

This book is a miracle! —a miracle in the sense that it appreciates what the Host is doing. Combines humility and humour, a gentle approach with firm convictions, and a loving attitude.
—Henrik Sonne Petersen, secretary general, Danish Mission Council

A strong call to follow Jesus, who related to those on the margins.
—Paul Nisly, professor emeritus, Messiah University

A gift of theological, ethical, missiological, and best of all, personal reflection. Story after story make vivid and accessible a compelling horizon for the embodiment of virtues like hospitality, mutuality, and nonviolence.
—Rev. Jeff Liou, PhD, national director of theological formation, InterVarsity Christian Fellowship/USA

This book is peppered with one-line zingers. "The diagnosis is not good for the American church." "Mission must be pacifist. And pacifism must be missional." "We tend to think that religious centers help us to be better disciples. But if anything, religious centers impede us." Peter Sensenig is not, however, interested in literary candy. He wants a change of behavior. Transformation. If you are interested in seeing your Muslim neighbor differently, this book is for you. And if you're not, read it anyway. You might be inspired to begin the "guestwork" the author is calling for.

—James R. Krabill, core adjunct faculty, Anabaptist Mennonite Biblical Seminary

Hospitality—and not just the positive encounters—has the power to bridge diversity and even resolve conflicts. You will enjoy the "Worst Field Trip Ever."

—Donna Kampen Entz, Mennonite worker, Burkina Faso

This book opened my heart. It invites readers into a way of hospitality that transforms hostility into friendship and reveals Jesus' good news at the edges.

—Rebeka Moeljono, MACF, spiritual director

Provocatively claims that the spiritual vitality of the church depends upon building relationships with Muslims—and offers hope for shalom. Compels me to ask: Who are the Muslims, or other strangers, with whom I might become a good guest?

—Rev. Dr. James Rissler

Concrete and moving examples of taking hospitality further, in the way of Jesus.

—Max P. Wiedmer, director, *Transmission*

Rarely does one have the opportunity of hearing from an academic in the trenches. But *Good Guestwork* is one such book. In this distillation of the stories and reflections on those brave experiences—far from the "ivory tower"—we gasp, weep, laugh, and marvel. And we are invited, indeed impelled, to see Jesus and join him in weakness and miracle on the uncomfortable and vulnerable margins.

—Jewel Showalter, service worker in Kenya, Middle East, and China; communications and development, Rosedale Bible College

A fresh framework for thinking about and guiding Christian engagement with Islam.

—R. Bruce Yoder, PhD, former executive coordinator, Africa Inter-Mennonite Mission

Through stimulating stories and memorable moments, *Good Guestwork* gives us a multitude of clues and examples to follow. Let's give it a try wherever we find ourselves!

—Larry Miller, general secretary emeritus, Mennonite World Conference; former secretary, Global Christian Forum

Succinctly captures the essential principle of the Kingdom of God: relationship building.

—Rev Dr. Paul Wose Mokake, director of evangelism and missions, Cameroon Baptist Convention

I highly recommend this book as an antidote to Christian approaches to Muslims that are either aggressive or believe we have nothing to offer.

—Ann Graber Hershberger, executive director, Mennonite Central Committee U.S.

This joyful book invites the reader to a paradigm-shifting realignment of our place in the mission of God.

—Jonathan Bornman, PhD, filmmaker, *Unexpected Peace*

Accessible and practical, yet theoretically rich and carefully researched.

—Nicholas R. Brown, Loyola Marymount University

A compassionate and deeply personal appeal... Highly recommended and warmly inviting!
—Philip A. Gottschalk, associate professor, Baptist Theological Institute, Bucharest, Romania

Blending accessible theology with vivid stories that show how friendships bear crucial witness to God's peace in a world aching for wholeness.
—Rev. Dr. Bethany McKinney Fox, author of *Disability and the Way of Jesus: Holistic Healing in the Gospels and the Church*

Clearly focused on Christian-Muslim relations, but with concepts that apply just as well to interactions with any ideological "other."
—Tim Huber, *Anabaptist World*

GOOD GUESTWORK

GOOD GUESTWORK

Christians and Muslims as Guests and Hosts

PETER M. SENSENIG

SANTOS BOOKS
EVERY STORY SACRED

Cover design: Ron Tinsley
First Printing, 2025
Published by Santos Books, LLC, Elizabethtown, PA 17022
Conrad Kanagy, Executive Editor/CEO
ISBN: 979-8-9994186-5-4

To Christy,
whose good guestwork is a joy to observe.

And to Felix, Celeste, and Musa,
the best guests we could hope for.

CONTENTS

Part I: Becoming Guests

CHAPTER 1

We Need...Muslims?

YOU NEED CHAD.

The massive billboard almost made me screech to a halt in the middle of the highway. It turns out Chad is just a lawyer who wants to help you if you have a car accident. I almost needed Chad the lawyer simply because of how distracting his huge billboard was.

But the reason I was taken aback was that I was on home assignment while serving in the central African country with the same name--Chad. As I drove, I was reflecting on the challenges of living in that country. I was asking myself, do I really fit there? Does my family? What am I really contributing? Does Chad need me?

YOU NEED CHAD.

Why do I need Chad? I stick out like a sore thumb--as a wealthy foreigner, as an English speaker, as a Christian service worker. What do I need from Chad?

This book is about why we *all* need Chad. I am convinced that the spiritual vitality of the church depends upon building relationships with Muslims.

Do you want to deepen your faith? Engage with Muslims who disagree with you.

Do you want to revitalize your church? Welcome Muslims who need your help.

Do you want the written Word of God to come alive? Notice the Samaritans around you.

Do you want the church to be committed to nonviolence? Befriend Muslims who remind you why you follow the Prince of Peace.

Do you want to be freed from the empty pursuit of wealth? Engage with Muslims who show you a different kind of treasure.

This book is about the *why* and *how* of that engagement. I call it *good guestwork*--the quest to become good guests and hosts of each other. And in turn to become God's guests.

YOU NEED CHAD might be one the most revolutionary things one could say today. It flies in the face of the ideology of separation that produces travel bans. The Chadian people made the list of twelve nationalities that the United States government decided it did *not* need. In response, the Chadian government declared, *We don't need you either*.

That's us--that's our family--left without visas to continue in the country where God called us. The place where our children feel at home, attend school, and raised a beloved stray kitten into a cat. The place where we learned languages, formed friendships and colleagues, and made our home.

It's not surprising that cynical politicians use fear to shore up support.

But what a tragedy that Christians believe them! Where in Scripture, the person of Jesus, the early church, or the work of the Holy Spirit, do we find the idea that we become better Christians by creating walls of separation?

On the contrary--if the biblical story is also our story,[1] then we must always be asking how to become guests and hosts of one another. As Ephesians 2:14 tells us, walls of separation are the enemy of Christ--and the good news is that he breaks down barriers.

The good news is not just *about* Jesus, but his *message* as well: the passage continues, "He came proclaiming good news to us: peace to those far away and to those near" (Eph 2:17).

The most profound expression of this good news that I've ever heard was spoken to me by a Muslim during my visit to Iran. He told me, "You are here because God sent you."

He did not just say, *I'm glad you are here.*

Or, *Let's do our best to be friends.*

No, he understood that *going in peace* is what God wants from us.

As I write this, hostility between Israel and Iran is erupting into mutual bombing.

The message of a bomb is simply this: we've calculated that the world would be better off without you. It's the exact antithesis of the hospitality of God, the creator of the world and the sustainer of life, to whom the whole earth belongs (Ps 24:1). God is the first and foremost example of what it means to *host*, to welcome strangers as friends, to make space for others (in the creative act, literally to make space out of nothing).

Hostility makes an idol of our own vision of the world, and who belongs in it. Do we want to be delivered from this idol? Then we need our Muslim neighbors. There's simply no other way.

Sibling rivalry

So why do we need each other as Christians and Muslims?

We can start with the big picture. Without peace between Muslims and Christians, the two largest faith communities in the world, there will be no world peace.[2] Displacement from war, forces of globalization, and urbanization put us in contact like never before.[3] Conflicts occur along Muslim-Christian lines. Why is this?

One reason is that we are engaged in what often looks like a *sibling rivalry*. A pastor in a majority-Muslim region of Ethiopia told me, "Muslims are our neighbors. We eat with them, we do business with them--we are like brothers and sisters."

At the same time, a Mennonite pastor in Tanzania struggled with the Muslim community around his church building. He lamented, "How can we make peace with Muslims when they have no interest in peace, only in violence and conquest?"

Siblings fight--and Muslims and Christians fight like siblings. Few things divide us more than what we have in common.[4] We are so *close* to one another, in the sense of sharing both theological and physical space. As the Ethiopian pastor insists, there is neighborly affection--rooted in our shared humanity and histories, in our communal life. The best impulses of faith reinforce this sibling love.

But we are also so *far away* from each other--and competition, politics, and violence erode trust that has been built. The intensity of these sibling encounters is not something we can ignore, simply hoping that it improves. People of both faiths must be active in reaching across the divide.

And where is this sibling interaction happening most intensely? *In Africa*. It is the only continent where the two faiths meet each other as equals--not only in terms of numbers, but also in the opportunities and challenges. For Christians in Africa, Islam is not just a religious system, it is about *people*. Muslims are not immigrants, aliens, or strangers. They are fellow citizens, neighbors, and family members. Ghanaian theologian John Azumah likens the two communities in Africa to two women married to one husband; "they bicker, they quarrel, sometimes they fight--but they just have to learn to live together. They cannot afford to see each other as enemies."[5]

If the analogy of siblings (or of wives married to the same man) is helpful, then part of the challenge is that these siblings are both motivated to share their faith. They are missionary religions--with the task of proclaiming that a prophetic message has changed the world forever.

What makes us look the most like siblings--the place where the family resemblance comes out the strongest, almost like looking in a mirror--is not theological. It is not religious practices. In beliefs and practices we are more like cousins.

No, where we are truly siblings is *in our missionary impulse*. It is the most important trait that we share. Christians and Muslims both hold to Martin Luther King, Jr.'s vision of a *great world house*--an intercultural human community meant to live as a single family of God.[6]

Are there rooms in this great world house where Christians don't often go?

The Christendom vision of the great world house is to divide up the rooms, so that it is clear who is in charge where. The closest thing to peace that we can hope for is to keep the siblings separated--since we're just going to fight anyway. The quest to establish Christian and Islamic territories reflects this vision of the world.

Good guestwork challenges this goal at its core. King's vision of an intercultural community of peace, justice, hope, and love is the exact opposite of territoriality. Good guestwork declares that we live in the great world house that God has created.

If there are rooms in this house that we fear are off limits--maybe that's exactly where God wants us to go.

We need...Muslims?

The big picture is helpful. But it's only a small part of why we need each other as Christians and Muslims. Loving in abstraction can only get us so far--the more important reality is what concrete encounter does to our faith.

Why do Christians need to become the guests of Muslims? Each chapter of this book answers this question in a different way.

Becoming guests reminds us that stories come first.

I begin with my experiences of becoming a guest in Somaliland, Chad, and Iran. Why stories? Because we sorely need to return theology to its proper place. Muslim-Christian encounters are *not* primarily about doctrines. We first meet each other as neighbors, with a joy that radiates from God and opens us up to the other. If we don't see Muslims first as people deserving the joy of God, we run the risk of never learning to trust and care for them.[7]

Sometimes Christians ask me, *What does Islam think about this issue?* My response is: Islam does not think--but Muslim people do. Why don't we ask them?

When Christy and I served in Zanzibar, the devotion of our Muslim neighbors to their faith was evident all around us. A neighbor of ours was the *muezzin* in the nearby mosque, and his voice called the neighborhood to prayer five times a day. His wife Maimuna is a warm and inviting person who prays faithfully and studies the Qur'an daily.

In the course of our friendship with Maimuna, Christy asked if she might have interest in studying Holy Scriptures together, with special attention to the Prophet Isa (the Arabic name for Jesus).

Maimuna's response was enthusiastic, but she wanted to clarify something from the outset: "What you really need to understand is that Jesus was *not* the son of God."

Was it our task to correct Maimuna's understanding of Jesus? Or was it first of all to enter into her life as *our* response to the incarnation?

It is encounters like this one that drew us to Zanzibar, and other places like it. Discipleship must be centered on entering into the everyday joys and struggles of people who are very different from us. It matters what we do with our bodies. Participating in God's love requires Christian bodies loving people concretely.[8]

If we have only ever considered Muslims in terms of doctrine, then we badly need the personal encounter. The opportunities abound--if we are only willing to step into some unfamiliar rooms.

Stepping out as a stranger is painful. These are not warm and fuzzy stories. We face crises of identity and belonging. We are confronted by the myths that have shaped us, for good or ill. Our faith and our hope are challenged at their core. Our love is tested.

But the pain--freely chosen for the sake of the gospel--is worth it. We end up finding Jesus in the most unexpected places. What Muslims offer Christians is a chance to encounter Jesus like never before. I met Jesus in Chad, and in Iran. Perhaps that's the message of this book. If it's the only thing you remember, I'll be satisfied.

But there's more.

Becoming guests of Muslims gives us skills of peacemaking.

There are some skills that we only learn from positions of vulnerability. And the overlap between these skills and kingdom discipleship is almost total.

Peace cells is the name I use for groups who are tuned in to the profound need for transformed relationships, precisely because they are in the minority. Christians in Burkina Faso, Palestine, and Indonesia, and Muslims in New York City--these groups show us how powerful peace cells really are.

Becoming guests of Muslims roots us deeper in Christ.

My home area in the US has an abundance of churches, large and small (and *mega*). Every time I return on home assignment there is a new mega-church whose name consists of one dynamic word, or starts with *The*.

The temptation can be to assume that my home area (and others like it) is a *center* of Christianity.

But here's the problem: *Christianity can have no centers*. It is a faith for strangers--exiles whose supreme loyalty is following Jesus. And where does Jesus lead? *Outside* the centers of power--unless it is to confront the powers like a lamb, and to offer up his life.

Who were the missionaries in the New Testament? Not the Jewish believers who stayed in Jerusalem, the geographical center of faith. The missionary church was in fact the culturally Greek Jews who were at home in the larger world. Did this fact make them less Jewish? No, it meant that they were *more* Jewish, because their Jewishness had been tested in the wider world. The fact that they had to stay Jewish in a pagan culture confirmed their commitment.[9]

We tend to think that religious centers help us to be better disciples. But if anything, religious centers impede us--if they make it more difficult for us to step out as guests of Muslims.

A life of exile seems dangerous on the surface. But in the words of Jesus, the far riskier option is to seek security: *Whoever wants to save their life will lose it. But whoever loses their life for me will find it* (Matt 16:25).

It is counterintuitive, but the more our spiritual life consists of being strangers, the more clearly we experience--and bear witness to--the gospel.

Our friend Maimuna--who happily agreed to read Scriptures together, but who wanted us first to understand that Jesus was *not* God incarnate--will never be convinced by clever arguments that somehow overwhelm her deeply held Islamic faith.

Nor will she be drawn to the power of Christian centers.

No--if Jesus' identity as the image of the invisible God is ever to become a reality to Maimuna, it will happen because she realizes that stepping into weakness, becoming a vulnerable stranger for the sake of relationship, is *fundamental to who God is*.

And how will she ever understand this unless she first encounters it in those who are committed to following Jesus? We all learn by analogy. Unless Christians first *become* the analogy of the incarnation, Jesus Christ will remain an abstraction--and therefore not worth engaging--for Muslims and many others.

Becoming guests of Muslims makes us better hosts.
Jesus liked giving tests to his disciples--lovingly and in hope.

One such test was when a Muslim woman wanted him to heal her demon-possessed daughter. He turns to his disciples and challenges their exclusionary thinking by putting it out in the open--their assumptions that salvation is for the Jews alone, that all others are like dogs. These comments are meant for the disciples, to test them. When he finally turns to the Muslim woman, he tenderly commends her faith and heals her daughter (Matt 15:21-28).[10]

Wait a minute, you say--there are no Muslims in the Bible! The woman was a Canaanite.

Well, yes. But if we cannot locate Muslims in the Bible, then our faith is meaningless. We are following some other gospel, not the good news of Jesus.

When we recognize this, we see Muslims all over the Bible. They are the Samaritans, the Canaanites, the Greeks, the Romans, the refugees and the vulnerable. This is what I call the *value of name-calling*. The Bible is more powerful in shaping our imagination than we realize--if we only let it do its work by putting ourselves in the story.

My doctoral mentor Glen Stassen liked to apply what he called the *historical fruits test*. How does our faith stand up to the pressing ethical challenges of our day? Does it bear Spirit fruit, or the bitter fruit of hostility and racism?[11] This is what Jesus was asking of his disciples when a Muslim woman came to him for help.

One of the most important tests of the quality of our faith is how we respond to the Muslim refugee crisis. How do we measure up?

The war in Sudan, starting in April 2023, has displaced millions internally and created over four million refugees in neighboring countries, including a million in Chad. How did the US government respond? By banning both Sudanese and Chadians from entering the country.

These are not opportunists--these are people fleeing from war, in need of refuge, being turned away by the wealthiest country in the world--a country with plenty of resources to help. Christians in the West should be repulsed by this apartheid kind of thinking. Are we?

Jesus is turning to us and making all the arguments we are tempted to make. What about our security? What about the economic cost? Shouldn't other countries be taking care of their own problems?

And yet, like the Canaanite woman, Muslim refugees are still there, waiting in hope. And Jesus stands ready to commend their faith and to heal.

The diagnosis is not good for the American church. It is tempting to lose heart, given the political and theological obstacles to seeing Jesus incarnated in the other, as he commands us to do in Matthew 25.

But there is hope when we look beyond the politicized rhetoric. A more profound test than political views or even voting patterns is the way in which churches actually respond to refugees' needs. Something beautiful is happening.

And the more that Christians become the guests of Muslims, the better the response when Muslims find themselves in need of help.

If we're going to pass this test, we'd better learn the skills of good guestwork.

Becoming guests of Muslims delivers us from half gospels.

What is a half gospel? One that leads the church away from the fullness of the Kingdom because of what it misses. As guests of Muslims we see the inadequacy of two half gospels in particular: personal salvation and social liberation. These half gospels resemble the kingdom of God. And that's because they are indeed the work of King Jesus. But they cannot stand alone.

A kingdom built on a radically nonviolent king crosses two divides. First, the chasm between Muslims and Christians, as we realize that the choice is not between established Christianity and Islam. Rather, the alternative is between the Kingdom of God and the kingdom of this world.

But a false choice also exists between progressive and conservative Christians--either you care about *peace* or you care about *evangelism*. No--the real options are the good news of the Messiah Jesus or the gospel of Mars, the god of war.

Mission must be pacifist. And pacifism must be missional. If we think we can have one without the other, we will discover just how easily other loyalties will fill the vacuum.

To be guests of Muslims is to discover how much we need a nonviolent Jesus, if we hope to touch and to share the kingdom of God.

And to be guests of Muslims is to realize that without the test of our religious rivals, our nonviolent commitments will be only surface-level.

As Randall Paul, my dialogue partner in Iran, likes to say, "Love your enemies, because they are so *useful*--to test your love."

What a gift our Muslim neighbors are offering us--a chance to shed our half gospels and embrace the fullness of the kingdom.

Becoming guests of Muslims helps us out of the trap of competition.

Christians in every context are wrestling with the question: What does mission look like? Even in places where Christians have historically been in the majority, they sense that they have been losing ground. It's an uncomfortable feeling--and can easily lead to fear and rivalry.

Our deliverance from the useless goal of winning requires going back to the vision and ethos of Jesus. It means finding a better way to interact. It means replacing competition with *mutuality*. The path of mutuality is one we can only walk alongside Muslims. Three major stepping stones along that path offer us solid ground.

To look *back with hope* is to recognize how much our relationships are improving.

To look *around with joy* means replacing our fear and shame with openness to the other.

And looking *forward with love* is to embrace the alternative to competition: inheriting the earth.

You would not know it from the news in the West, but Iranians are obsessed with friendship. Iranian scholars are producing books and articles by the dozen on the subject of friendship. Why the fascination? Because friendship is a radical form of resistance. They see it as the only hope for change in a political world gone mad.

They are not just talking about people who share their faith. One Ayatollah told me, "When I go abroad I am the guest of Christians from the beginning to the end of my journey."

Another described friendship as the highest form of salvation, and quoted a Muslim sage who declared, "If in the end I could receive all the blessings of God, but lose friendship--I would choose friendship."

There is a deep yearning for friendship and mutuality, if only we can find our way into each other's lives.

The past, present, and future of the Muslim-Christian relationship has tremendous promise. But we cannot do it alone.

Becoming guests of Muslims tunes us in to the miraculous.

The good news is that it is not up to us to make it happen. God, the Host of all of us, is working alongside, with, and before us. Our task is to recognize what he is doing.

Why does anyone come to Jesus? For transformation, for hope--for a miracle.

Is it an exaggeration to call the transformation of hostility a miracle? Yes--in the best possible way.

The value of exaggerated commitment

"Any story worth telling is worth exaggerating," stated Harry Truman.

The same is true of theology; anything worth saying about God is worth saying to the point of absurdity. To take it even further, anything worth stating about ourselves, our commitments, and one another is also worth *over*stating.

This book is full of exaggerations. Not untruths--because lies are never worth saying. To exaggerate, rather, is to home in on what one really cares about. To believe in something is to accept it for all its implications.

The Bible is not free of exaggeration. John concludes his Gospel with this statement: "Jesus did many other things as well. If every one of them were written down, I suppose that even the whole world would not have room for the books that would be written" (21:25). Precision is not the goal for John; rather, the intent is to portray the cosmic, all-pervasive importance of Jesus the Messiah.

Jesus lived an exaggerated life--in word and deed, pushing loyalties to their maximum capacity...and then demanding more. Parables, one of his main teaching methods, are exaggerated tales. And he described discipleship in the same overstated terms; "If anyone would follow me, let them deny themself and take up their cross and follow me" (Matt 16:24). He then observes that such a decision is worth more than "gaining the whole world" (v. 26). Really, Jesus? You've calculated the value of the *whole world* and determined that one person self-sacrificially giving you their allegiance to the point of death is worth more than that?

To be a disciple of Jesus means that we, along with the scribe who approached him, exaggerate our commitments: "Teacher, I will follow you wherever you go" (Matt 8:19). The disciples engaged in exaggerated commitments; Peter declares to Jesus, "Even if everyone else deserts you, I will never desert you" (Matt 26:33).

Why do we shy away from exaggeration? Perhaps we fear that by overstating, we give ourselves too much credit. Or that we give our *rivals* too much credit. Or that we risk being seen as naïve and idealistic. Maybe we worry that overstating one thing means understating something else, and therefore presents a warped version of the truth.

These are all legitimate concerns. But they are also telling; they all reveal that at the core of discipleship, under all the layers of religiosity and habit, is a kernel of self-doubt--about our motivations, our commitments, our worthiness. More than anything, we fear ourselves--fear that we will fail when our allegiance to Christ is put to the test. We fear that we are committing to more than we can deliver.

That's a good way to describe following Jesus: committing to more than we are sure we can deliver. The people who were a bit too calculating about their promises always managed to find some excuse: getting married, buying some land and some oxen, or burying a parent.

What Jesus demands, it seems, is a little bit of recklessness. The only occasion where he explicitly condemns reckless abandon is when Peter takes up his sword in defense of justice. The good news is that Jesus will never say no to a heart that says yes to him. Observe his response to Peter, who grossly overstated his commitment to his lord: "When you turn back to me, strengthen the others" (Luke 22:32). In other words, *You will get there. You will reach where you claimed to be going.*

Exaggerated commitment is one way to describe Christian calling.

Commitment to absolute pacifism.

Commitment to serving as ambassadors of Christ among Muslim people.

Commitment to losing the fight rather than trying to defeat the other--that loss is the only path to inherit the earth.

Commitment to seeing God at work in the world--that life-giving encounters between Muslims and Christians are nothing short of miracles.

And perhaps the most exaggerated claim of all--that we are actually God's guests, and God's partners, in kingdom work. We join the Holy Spirit's task of creating space for all of us.

There is no other path of discipleship besides exaggeration. This is because commitments are essential steps in our formation as disciples. We are--or at least eventually we become--who we say we are. We begin to care about what we claim to care about.

In other words, exaggeration is not a self-serving, untruthful act; it is rather the creative work of the Spirit calling us to a better kingdom than the one we already know. Unexpectedly, with such liberty the standard for truthful speech is higher, not lower. The only thing worth exaggerating is what was worth saying in the first place, bringing us always back to the question, "*Is this worth saying?*"

In the context of Muslim-Christian relations, much of what we might think important to say is actually excluded if we ask the simple question, "Is this worth saying?" Does it serve the purpose of transformed and renewed relationships? Does it reflect the in-breaking reign of God and the new humanity ushered in by Jesus on the cross (Eph 2:15)? Does it pull our commitments toward King Jesus and his gentle, serving, nonviolent reign?

The exaggerations here should be taken not as embellishment--the attempt to make something unattractive look beautiful--but rather as *reaching for the heart of what is beautiful about the good news*.

Perhaps another word for exaggerated commitment is *faith*. In the end, what we consider to be exaggerations turn out to be reality in God's kingdom. Our struggle to grasp the depth of *how good* is the good news we have received means that we are always catching up, trying to keep pace with our Host who goes ahead of us and beckons us into the Promised Land.

It's a long and sometimes painful journey--but there's joy on the way.

Let's jump in.

NOTES

[1] James Wm. McClendon, Jr., *Systematic Theology, Vol. 1: Ethics* (Nashville: Abingdon, 2002), 30-33.

[2] Miroslav Volf, Ghazi bin Muhammad, and Melissa Yarrington, eds., *A Common Word: Muslims and Christians on Loving God and Neighbor* (Grand Rapids, MI: Wm B. Eerdmans Publishing Co., 2010), 28.

[3] Martin Accad notes that the difficulty of coexistence leads us to gravitate toward religious ghettos that ignore each other's existence. Multi-faith societies like Lebanon offer special experience and wisdom for societies like Europe and the United States as they step into a multi-faith reality that the Middle East has lived for the past fourteen hundred years. *Sacred Misinterpretation: Reaching Across the Christian-Muslim Divide* (Grand Rapids, MI: Wm B. Eerdmans Publishing Co., 2019), 31.

[4] Lamin Sanneh, "Secular Values in the Midst of Faith: A Critical Discourse on Dialogue and Difference," in *Theology and the Religions: A Dialogue*, ed. Viggo Mortensen (Grand Rapids, MI: Wm B. Eerdmans Publishing Co., 2003), 137.

[5] John Azumah, "Toward Cordial Witness among Muslims: An African Perspective: Through the Lens of Historical Relations," November 8, 2007, Fuller Theological Seminary Missiology Lectures (podcast). Cited in Evelyne A. Reisacher, *Joyful Witness in the Muslim World* (Grand Rapids, MI: Baker Academic, 2016), 35.

[6] Hak Joon Lee, *The Great World House: Martin Luther King, Jr. and Global Ethics* (Cleveland: Pilgrim, 2011), xi-xii.

[7] Reisacher, *Joyful Witness*, 157.

[8] Willie James Jennings, *The Christian Imagination: Theology and the Origins of Race* (New Haven, CT: Yale University Press, 2010), 167.

[9] John Howard Yoder, *Theology of Mission: A Believers Church Perspective*, ed. Gayle Gerber Koontz and Andy Alexis-Baker (Downers Grove, IL: IVP Academic, 2014), 82, 86.

[10] Munther Isaac, *The Other Side of the Wall: A Palestinian Christian Narrative of Lament and Hope* (Downers Grove, IL: InterVarsity, 2020), 44-46.

[11] Glen Harold Stassen, "Prologue : testing ethical method in the laboratory of history," in *Justice and the Way of Jesus: Christian Ethics and the Incarnational Discipleship of Glen Stassen*, David P. Gushee and Reggie L. Williams, eds. (Maryknoll, NY: Orbis, 2020).

CHAPTER 2

Pain and Joy in Guesting

"Hey! Are you CIA?" a man called across the street to me in Somaliland.

"No!" I replied. Cars rushed between us.

"Are you sure?" he asked, with a grin on his face. I laughed.

Pretty sure. I think that's something I'd be aware of.

The question behind the question was: Then who *are* you?

It is exhausting to live with that question, day in and day out, on people's lips, in their eyes, in the name-calling and assumptions. We don't usually think of guests as feeling the need to justify their presence. A guest is a person who is welcomed, shown a level of honor and respect, whose presence is assumed to bring something of value. But when we frame mission in terms of good guestwork, we are forced to recognize that becoming strangers for the sake of Jesus, as often as not, provokes suspicion. We are not received as welcome guests, but as a potential or actual threat.

Our natural response to finding ourselves in this kind of situation is, What am I doing here? The pain can be intense--existential, lonely, crushing. But this is precisely the gift that guests bring. Just as religious minorities are in a particular position to develop peacemaking skills, so also guests have a special gift for sensing hidden pain.

Henri Nouwen describes the process of healing as moving from *your* pain to *the* pain.[1] When our focus turns inward on the circumstances of our own pain, we become angry and resentful. So Jesus' prayer on the cross, "Father forgive them, for they don't know what they are doing," was the move from *his* pain into all of humanity's pain. When we realize that our particular pain is part of all humanity's pain, it is easier to bear.

The calling to live in solidarity with those who suffer, astonishingly, becomes the easy yoke that Jesus promised. Through contact with the hungry, the homeless, the refugees, the prisoners, and the sick, *our* pain is turned toward *the* pain. Paradoxically, the path that runs through *the* pain is the way to joy.

Those who follow Jesus as strangers in a strange land will suffer. Part of the reason is that foreigners are easy targets for hostility. But a deeper reason is that guests are forced into circumstances where they must turn their attention from *their* pain to *the* pain. Retaliation is not a viable option. Neither is it possible to turn to self-loathing, saying, "I don't belong here--this pain is my fault for simply being here." No. We have to do something with the hurt, if we're going to continue as a guest.

And when we make that shift--from our pain to the pain--we are able to notice all of the suffering that happens below the surface, boiling like a pressure cooker with no outlet for the steam. We notice families struggling economically and relationally. We see sickness, sometimes hidden in shame from the community. We see frustration and hopelessness in the face of corruption, poverty, and abuse, with no solution in sight.

Often it takes an outsider to see these things, and to respond. To be present where you are not wanted but have something to offer is prophetic.[2] We are not guests because we are warmly welcomed, but because God has called us to be guests.

For every story a service worker tells with a happy ending, there are ten untold stories of pain. We may be drawn to the accounts of danger and self-sacrifice--but not if they end with hurt. So these stories are left untold, and we all miss out. It's unfortunate, because these are the stories of moving from *our* pain to *the* pain, and we need to hear them.

Identity crisis

I was brought into the Mennonite story in Somalia when my parents, J. Carl and Julia Sensenig, served for three years in Mogadishu with Eastern Mennonite Board of Missions and Charities (now called EMM).

By the time my family arrived in Mogadishu, the Mennonite-Somali story was already more than three decades old. Mennonites had served in Somalia through periods of colonial authority and independence. Schools and hospitals nationalized. They were dismissed from the country when it took a socialist turn. Later they were welcomed back when the political winds shifted.

Mogadishu was a cosmopolitan city. The Italian colonial influence was evident in the architecture, language, and pasta. To this day I consider Somali *baasto* (spaghetti) to be the tastiest in the world. I seek it out in Nairobi, Minneapolis, Djibouti, and Atlanta; it arrives with a banana and plenty of green hot sauce.

I experienced Somalis as gregarious and warm, with affection for children. On one occasion my family was strolling through the fish market along the coast. I lagged behind the rest, enjoying the beautiful displays of captured sea life--rays, sharks, squid, and countless fish of various shapes and colors.

One fish-monger, noting my appreciation for his wares, offered me a small brightly-colored fish. Knowing my older brothers' tendency to relieve me of my most prized possessions, usually by wily manipulation, I slipped the precious fish into the pocket of my shorts.

Then I promptly forgot about it.

The shorts made it into a drawer, where the Mogadishu heat began to do its work. Within a day the house started to smell a bit funky, and by the following day the whole place reeked of death.

Intensive interrogation and a thorough search uncovered the source of the stench. My attempts to blame it on the kindness of a stranger fell on deaf ears.

On another occasion, I surprised a well-to-do Somali couple strolling near our house. On a dare from my older brother, I jumped out of a tree in front of them and requested *baksheesh*, a charitable donation often granted during the month of Ramadan. My request was successful, as the man dug in his pocket with an amused expression on his face. I count the coin as one of the many gifts I owe to Somalis.

My brothers and I attended the American School of Mogadishu, with classmates and teachers from Somalia and from all over the globe. We engaged in sporting events with other national or international schools around the city.

On Fridays we attended church in the Catholic cathedral, where the Mennonite service workers worshiped along with Somalis who had found faith in Christ. Often this meant some degree of estrangement from their families and social circles.

My brothers and I were mostly shielded from the turmoil that was descending upon the country. We heard scattered gunfire. We overheard the staff of Mennonite Mission (including Mennonite Central Committee) and other organizations discussing the impact of the conflict on Somali friends and institutions. The small Christian minority was being targeted and many lost their lives.

The 1988 genocide in northern Somalia, known as Somaliland, at the hands of the Siad Barre regime led Western aid donors to cut off funding. In the summer of 1989 my family, like many of the expatriates and Somalis who had the means, left Mogadishu. Rebel groups surrounded the city, and eventually toppled the dictator. A protracted civil war enveloped Somalia.

For years the news was devastating. War led to famine, and famine led to more conflict. Refugees fled to Kenya and to wherever they could find shelter around the world.

The U.S. was buoyed by the triumph of the Cold War. They were the guardians of a new world order, and collaborated with the United Nations to send peacekeeping forces to Somalia. But the optimism of an international peace led by the West quickly eroded. The Black Hawk Down incident in October 1993 signaled the end of that narrative.

I maintained an interest in Somalia even as our family shifted to life in the United States. But my contact was limited to news articles, reunions for former service workers in Somalia, and the occasional visit from a Somali guest.

My dormant interest was rekindled, however, when I fell in love with Christy in graduate school. She had spent time in Muslim communities in West Africa, and she agreed to marry me on the condition that we pursue international ministry together as soon as possible.

The hottest fart in the world

So we began to explore possibilities. When Mennonites were forced to leave Somalia in the early 1990s, they pursued other ways of staying engaged in the region, including an office in Nairobi. EMM also established a presence in the small arid nation of Djibouti. Djibouti is a crossroads of Somali, Afar, Arab, and other peoples, with strategic military bases for the US and for its former colonists, the French.

A few months after we were married, Christy and I joined another EMM couple who were well established in Djibouti. I taught English courses in the language department of the University of Djibouti, and Christy worked with the culturally diverse Protestant church and as a community health volunteer in a refugee camp.

In Djibouti we encountered a unique majority-Somali society shaped by French culture, Arab influences, and countless connections with the West. It was fascinating and attractive--and with a climate so harsh it complicated every aspect of life.

I was learning French. I began describing Djibouti in conversation-- or so I thought--as "the hottest country in the world." Unfortunately, the French words for *country* and for *fart* are close enough for a beginner to confuse the two. Imagine my embarrassment when I realized I had been going around saying that Djibouti was the "hottest fart in the world." To their credit, no one seemed too offended.

In the extreme heat we boarded a bus one day and heard a voice from the back: "Get me out of this **** country." It was not a Somali voice. It was not American. It was distinctly Irish. The fun adventure across Africa that this young man was imagining had hit a wall in Djibouti. It was too hot to think or to do much of anything but sweat.

I have used his tagline on occasion myself.

During the hottest part of the year the city was wracked by power cuts. We would watch the fan stop moving, and moments later a cacophony of generators belching smoke would start up all around us. It blended with the call to prayer from a dozen minarets. It was so loud you could barely think.

How could one possibly hear the voice of Jesus in such an environment?

In Djibouti I was introduced to Somali converts to Christian faith. They gathered in small groups around their newfound religious identities. I met regularly to study the Bible with two Somali men. One of them was facing severe reactions from his family, including violent beatings.

These men's dedication to their faith and eagerness to learn was invigorating. We studied the Sermon on the Mount together. Jesus' promise of joy for those who are persecuted because of him cut directly to our hearts.

I have never forgotten what I learned in those moments. The standard of faith is not the comfortable Christian who attends church and lives a godly, generous, and predictable life, as fruitful as this may be.

No. The kind of faith described in the Sermon on the Mount makes little sense to outsiders. This faith is expressed in difficult and costly choices, whose only explanation is that one has heard the voice of Jesus.

Another young man flagged me down on the street in Djibouti. He told me that he had encountered Jesus in a dream. Would I be willing to talk with him about it?

I was surprised. I had no idea who this person was, but I accepted and we read from the Bible and prayed together. Years later, I learned that this man had gone to Ethiopia for mission training, with the goal of returning to preach the good news to his people.

Someone heard Jesus through all the noise.

Though more stable than Somalia, Djibouti was not untouched by the trauma of war. Refugee camps were full of people fleeing the conflict; how could so many displaced people either integrate in a new place or return to a context that they barely recognized, with no means to make a life?

Murder, maiming, and Mennonite mission

From Djibouti I entered a PhD program at Fuller Theological Seminary, with a concentration in Christian ethics. When it came time to choose a dissertation topic, I realized that the subject I most wanted to explore was the Mennonite peacemaking presence in Somalia.

The place to start my research was with former Mennonite service workers. I conducted a dozen interviews of people who had served in Somalia, from the very beginning of the work in the early 1950s, to the more recent academic partnerships in Somaliland.

Two stories in particular emerged as important from the early years of the Somali Mennonite Mission. After the Mennonite schools had been operating for several years, a Somali man who had become radicalized through Egyptian extremists attacked and killed a Canadian Mennonite teacher named Merlin Grove.

He also stabbed Merlin's wife Dorothy, who survived the attack. At the trial, Dorothy publicly forgave her husband's killer. She later returned to Somalia to serve again. Many Somalis expressed deep sympathies for the tragedy. They were profoundly moved by the display of forgiveness, and by the fact that the Mennonites continued to serve in the country.

In 1963, one year after the murder of Grove, the Somali national assembly banned the teaching of any religion other than Islam. The government declared that even Christian-run schools were obligated to teach Islam. The Mennonites, who were there for the sake of Christian witness, faced a crisis. Should they teach a rival religion in their school?

Another organization decided to close its schools rather than include Islam in the curriculum. Mennonite Mission put the question to the bishops in the United States, and also asked the Somali Christians to advise them. Their answer was clear: Continue to run the schools with Islam as a subject of study. Muslim teachers were hired to teach classes on Islam.

These two incidents have had a long life in Somali collective memory. Because of the decision to stay, the Mennonite schools exercised significant influence in the country through the education of many Somali students. It communicated to Somalis that the Mennonite Mission was respectful toward Islam. According to one Mennonite worker, decades later Somalis told him that they could trust the Mennonites because they stayed. They were not simply there to win numbers, but sincerely cared about Somalis.

Clan is an important and well-known identity marker for Somalis. A common Somali proverb puts it this way: "Me and my clan against the world. Me and my family against my clan. Me and my brother against my family. Me against my brother."

When Mennonites came to Somalia, they represented the beginning of something new: a clan not founded on blood relations. A clan based on a commitment to making peace with strangers and even enemies.

So even before Mennonites were using the language of peacemaking, they were facilitating peaceful coexistence between clans in the Mennonite schools. Fighting between clans was not tolerated, and as a result clan differences were never pronounced or even very visible.

In the classrooms and the dormitories the students established friendships across clans. They learned the value of peace, and that formation stayed with them for the rest of their lives. Identities were shifting, stretching the given categories. They began to refer to themselves as the *Somali Mennonites*.

As Somalia devolved into civil war, these individuals bore witness to the Kingdom of God that transcends ethnic and family ties. Along with the Mennonite service workers who had left their families and communities behind in North America, these Somalis made up a peace cell with a new identity as peacemakers.

Mennonites played a modest role in encouraging peacebuilding meetings between clan elders. The goal was to preserve traditional structures. This *from the ground up* approach describes well the Anabaptist posture in all kinds of areas--theology, church practices, peacebuilding, social change.

One important practitioner of this kind of approach was Ahmed Haile.[3] Haile studied peace theology at a Mennonite seminary. He returned to Somalia at great risk to negotiate peace. At one meeting, an explosion took his leg and nearly his life. An outspoken Christian, he was nevertheless respected as a peacemaker by his fellow Somalis.

Peace cells challenge identity markers. The results can be transformative--but it's a dangerous business. Even mentioning the possibility of a Somali Christian is risky, as I was later to find out for myself.

Myth meets pain: Somaliland

I had been immersed in this story from childhood. It was so compelling to me that I wrote my dissertation about it.

The stories rose to the level of myth. A myth is not untrue--it's a powerful narrative that shapes the way one sees the world.

So it's not surprising that I started to imagine that I could be a part of this special relationship.

From Mennonite workers I was hearing stories like this one: A Kenyan friend decided to go to Somaliland as a Christian teacher. He made contact and secured a job. When officials discovered that he was a Christian they asked what kind of a Christian he was. They told him, "If you are Mennonite, you can come."

Another story I was told: Two Mennonite teachers visited Somaliland. The Minister of Education begged them to send teachers. A Somali man sitting beside them leaned over and whispered, "We don't want just any teachers; we want *Mennonite* teachers."

Wow! We can do something special with this kind of invitation!

On top of this, there was an exciting partnership between my alma mater and a university in Hargeisa, to establish a peace institute. How fitting--and just right for a newly minted PhD. I paid a visit and got a warm welcome from the president of the university.

Christy made contact with a well-known hospital run by the former first lady of the country. She arranged to work as a maternity nurse.

We were up front with everyone that we were with Mennonite Mission. Be authentic--and you will find surprising goodwill and space to operate. This was the lesson of the Mennonite legacy in Somalia. And it seemed to be well received by the Somali Muslims we met.

Full of dreams and driven by such a powerful myth, we made plans to move to Somaliland with our three-year-old son. We raised support for a term with EMM, telling ourselves, *We'll start with three years and go from there.*

Surely this is such a perfect fit that we'll make a career out of it.

For a brief moment, the myth held.

We were met in Hargeisa by two men named Ahmed and Hussein. Ahmed had been a teacher in the Mennonite schools nearly forty years earlier. Hussein had been a student at the same school. They took us under their protection, and introduced us to people. They became our advocates at the university and the hospital and in our neighborhood. They visited us and checked to make sure we had everything we needed. They treated us like their own children and our son like their grandson. Before we arrived in Somaliland we had never met these two Somali men. Yet somehow we were *their people*. They understood that Mennonites believed in peace, and they identified with that way of being in the world.

With the help of Hussein and Ahmed, we began the hard work of building a life in Hargeisa. We put our son in a small school. Christy started working as a nurse at Edna Adan Hospital. I taught courses at the peace institute. One course I co-taught along with a former ambassador. A previous vice president of Somaliland was a student in that course.

My colleagues and students were warm and receptive. I began to imagine the coming years taking shape--learning Somali language, building deep friendships, continuing the Mennonite story in Somalia.

The myth gave us a sense of power. We felt we could overcome any obstacles we encountered.

Children threw rocks at us in the street. *No matter, kids will be kids.*

A group of young men mugged Christy in front of our son, grabbing her arm and threatening her with a big rock--*Well, there* is *a lot of desperation and poverty around.*

People we didn't know told us to go back to where we came from, to get out of their country--*I guess you can find Trumpism anywhere in the world.*

The university asked us to keep an armed guard at our house--*Perhaps this is just the form their hospitality takes.*

We were sure we could handle it, because pushing on through was part of the myth. You don't get to joy without pain, to real relationships without the discomfort of being a vulnerable stranger. I didn't realize how much opposition to our presence was building under the surface.

On the first day of a new course at the university, my first course without a co-teacher, a middle-aged student stood up.

"Where did you study?" he asked.

"Fuller, in California," I told him.

"It's a Christian university?" he said.

"Yes."

"So what are you doing here? We don't need anything from Christians. I also looked up your parents--they were Christians working in Somalia. Somalis don't want people like you here."

I was crestfallen. All the goodwill I'd built at the peace institute seemed to be crumbling around me. I tried to continue, but the student kept interrupting me. He promised me, "I'm not going to allow you to teach--and there are other students here who agree with me."

He held up some documents and turned to the rest of the class. "I have information about this man right here." The other thirty students sat watching in silence to see how I would respond. One or two of them told the confrontational man to sit down.

My heart racing, I managed to finish the session. But I left the classroom shaken and unsure of my future there. I would ask for a meeting with the president in the morning to figure out what was going on.

As it turns out, I didn't have to request a meeting. The next morning I was called before the university president and the entire administrative staff.

The president got right to the point. He pulled out an article that I had published, which referred to Ahmed Haile as a Somali Christian peacemaker.

"Did you write this?" he demanded. I confirmed that I had.

He informed me that the article was being circulated by the student who had confronted me. "Also," he said, "your name is being published on social media. Al-Shabaab is active in the neighborhood where you are living."

The president did not look me in the eye. "My advice to you is that you leave the country within ten days. You are not safe here. Until you leave you will have to have an armed guard with you at all times."

In a daze I called Christy and told her the news. I arrived home to find the local police had posted guards at our gate.

Within a few days we said goodbye to friends and colleagues and flew to Kenya. We had been in Hargeisa only two and a half months.

The hurt and disappointment were sharp. We had been planning this move for years in advance, including tailoring our education toward this goal. We were ready to do the work of making this cross-cultural leap. We were in it for the long haul--we had no other plan.

And it was all gone in a moment. At least that's what it felt like.

How was it possible that God had called us there, only to have our service cut short so suddenly? Had we indeed heard the voice of God?

"What did you expect?"

This was the response of a French friend when he heard our story. He was someone who grew up in church but had left his faith behind.

"You show up in a Muslim country as Christians. You try to change their culture and religion. Of course they are going to respond to you like that."

At this point we were located in Kenya, trying to figure out where to go next. We were disoriented and confused--and perhaps a bit embarrassed about how confidently we had shared with our supporting communities what we felt God calling us to do.

Our friend had put his finger right on our insecurity. Was calling just a word we used for what we wanted to do? For the pressure to live into a particular story? For idealism in a world that calls for a bit more realistic caution?

We found ourselves using the words of the disciples on the road to Emmaus. Jesus met them as they walked, but they didn't recognize him. *We had hoped*, they told Jesus.

Over those months we uttered that phrase many times--*We had hoped*. Should we return to the US, look for something else? Or look for another location in Africa?

All we could do was say to Jesus what the disciples said on the road to Emmaus--stay with us. Don't leave us confused and alone.

From Kenya we discerned our next steps. We spent time in Eastleigh, the Somali neighborhood of Nairobi. We visited other parts of the region, praying about where we should go. God led us to Zanzibar, Tanzania.

But the connection to Somaliland had not ended. There was still an open door, particularly for me to keep up the relationship with two different universities.

So I returned to Somaliland three times to offer short courses and seminars. I was joined on two of these occasions by Mennonite professors from the US who had significant experience in the Horn of Africa, Mike Brislen from James Madison University and Jonathan Rudy from Elizabethtown College.

On each visit, I was struck again by the warmth of the reception we were given, the thoughtfulness of the students, and the power of the friendships we had made in the Horn years before. A measure of healing took place with each sojourn.

I will never know the full circumstances of our sudden departure from Somaliland. But I did learn a few details later.

One was that the university president himself was on the defensive. He had spent thirty years in New Jersey before moving back to Somaliland. There was conflict between those who stayed in Somaliland and the returning diaspora. This put him in an embattled and vulnerable position. He could not use valuable social capital to defend my presence at the university.

Another was that a professor whom I barely knew was unhappy that I was there. He was behind the student resistance that came to a head in the classroom that day.

On top of all this, Somaliland moves periodically between orientation toward the Arab world and toward the West. Our arrival in Hargeisa happened just as the pendulum was swinging more toward the Arabian Peninsula. The hostility toward Westerners that we experienced was at least somewhat related to this.

Does all of this ease the pain of *we had hoped*, of having one's offer of friendship so fiercely rejected? Not entirely.

But it does help me move from *my* pain to *the* pain. The rejection that we felt is our participation in the suffering of others.

By showing up in Somaliland, Christy and I touched the pain of war, displacement and return, ethnic rivalry, and powerlessness that Somalis experience.

And it was preparation for what was to come.

NOTES

[1] Henri J.M. Nouwen, *The Inner Voice of Love* (New York: Doubleday, 1996), 103.

[2] Shabrae Jackson Krieg and Janet Balasiri Singleterry, editors, *Voices Rising: Women of Color Finding and Restoring Hope in the City*, Kindle edition (Pomona, CA: Servant Partners, 2018), location 2315.

[3] Ahmed Ali Haile (as told by David Shenk), *Teatime in Mogadishu: My Journey as a Peace Ambassador in the World of Islam* (Harrisonburg, VA: Herald, 2011).

CHAPTER 3

Meeting Isa in Chad and Iran

After five years in Zanzibar, we sensed a call to move into French-speaking Africa. Part of what we heard God saying was that our gifts and training could be useful in the poorest part of the world, where relatively few service workers are sent.

So we spent a year in France to prepare and to get our children into the French school system.

We moved to the central African country of Chad and were impressed by the resilience and hospitality of Chadians. But we were also immediately confronted by the need. Severe flooding put large sections of the capital city under water, including the seminary where I was planning to teach. The first course I led took place in a little church building with a dirt floor and no electricity. Books, buildings, and budget were all lost to the floodwaters.

A political crisis left dozens dead or disappeared, and a whole country reeling. Coups and militia violence in surrounding countries raised the constant question: is Chad next?

War in neighboring Sudan brought a million refugees into eastern Chad.

Christy regularly saw mothers and babies dying in childbirth at the hospital. Death--often with no explanation, by Western standards--was just a part of the lives of our Chadian friends. They asked us for help--with hospital bills, house repairs, and school tuition.

And in the midst of it all, we found meaning and joy in our work and relationships. One of the bright points in my life was teaching with my colleague Sali. For two years we planned courses together and shared the classroom sessions. *I can see this working for a long time*, I thought. Sali helped me understand the central African context. I nudged him toward a theology of peacemaking. It was a terrific collaboration.

Then one day Sali announced that he was returning to his native Cameroon to take a position there.

I felt stranded. I asked God to show me where I should put my efforts. How could I best encourage and join the Muslim-Christian peacebuilding work to which God had called me?

At this low point, I found myself praying for an encouraging breakthrough--either in the work that I've been involved in, or in something new altogether.

As I was praying, I got a call from Pastor Victor. In the previous years I'd worked with him on Muslim-Christian dialogue, sponsored by Mennonite Central Committee. We'd traveled together to central Chad to encourage interfaith peace committees, and to lead youth seminars on multi-faith peacebuilding.

Pastor Victor was calling to invite me to an event where he was speaking. The event was entitled "National Week of Peaceful Cohabitation." Pastor Victor was addressing the role of religious leaders in promoting social cohesion in Chad.

This is just the thing, I thought. This event would yield some encouraging new relationships. It will offer me a fresh vision for peacebuilding in Chad.

I arrived on time, and a large group had gathered on the campus. Some were waiting in line for lunch, and I looked around for Pastor Victor. I did not see anyone I knew. But I was encouraged by the large group of Muslims and Christians who had gathered for such an event, and who seemed to be enjoying themselves together.

There were people with cameras around, and so I also pulled out my phone and snapped an informal photo of the group. I was well aware that cameras are off-limits in some places in Chad, particularly those related to the military or police. But this was an interfaith event in an enclosed campus, and so I assumed that it was a safe place.

I was immediately confronted by a Muslim man (who was not in the photo himself), who grabbed my hand, snatched my phone, and yelled in my face, "What are you going to do with that? Erase it now!"

Shocked, I said, "I'm sorry, I'll delete it right away." Not knowing what else to do, I held out my hand with the Islamic greeting, "Assalaam aleikum."

He said angrily, "You don't greet me."

I was aware that dozens of people around us were observing the interaction. To try to reinforce that I had only goodwill, I repeated the greeting.

With extreme anger on his face he shouted, "You are the reason for all of Chad's suffering, you French."

When he finally allowed me to get a word in, I said, "But I'm not French."

"Well, what nationality are you then?"

"American."

"It's the same thing. Get out of our country!"

I was blindsided. To be confronted like this at a celebration of peaceful cohabitation between faiths! With my heart racing, I tried to explain that I'd been invited by one of the speakers to this event. He shouted, "I don't care--you're here to film."

"No, I came to..."

"Liar! I saw you taking a picture."

"I didn't come to film, I came to promote peace."

He repeated, "But it's you who cause all of Chad's suffering. Get out of here."

I looked around. No one had stepped in to try to mediate the situation. I felt utterly alone, attacked, misunderstood, humiliated, with my already fragile hope trampled underfoot. I couldn't understand why no one was coming to the defense of the only foreigner to show up to this event. It was as if there was tacit agreement, by both Muslims and Christians alike, with what he was shouting at me.

I nearly followed the man's advice and left then and there. But I'd already told Pastor Victor that I had arrived. I couldn't bail on him now. I summoned the courage to stay, and eventually Pastor Victor appeared. We went into the hall where the speaking session was to be held. I did not tell him what had just happened, as I recognized that he was already in a challenging position, as a Christian speaking publicly in a Muslim-majority environment. I could not ask him to navigate my circumstances in addition to what he was already bearing.

The session itself was positive--or at least it would have been if the calls for peaceful coexistence had not rung hollow in my ears, traumatized as I was by what had just happened.

On my way back to catch a taxi home, jumping over mud puddles, I tried to make some sense of it. I was reeling, with the serious question on my heart as to whether it would be possible to continue in Chad. The cheerful greetings of children playing in the streets lifted my heart a little.

In the days following, I tried to process this confrontation and make some sense of it. I called up a few trusted friends, including Chadians. As I talked it through, I realized that the incident had triggered my earlier experiences in Somaliland. To be told by strangers that we were unwanted was linked in my mind to eventually being forced to leave. The same questions about whether my family is safe in this context were brought to the surface. In my embodied memory there was a link between these kinds of confrontations and the real security of a situation.

The Somaliland experience had taught me that the key to getting through this was moving from *my* pain to *the* pain. The anger that this man showed spoke to some deep pain that he has not been able to address. I disciplined myself to pray for his healing, and to ask God to shower him with good things.

But what was behind his pain? Part of the challenge is that it is impossible to know how pervasive his attitude is. I felt betrayed by the people who had observed the incident, and said nothing. Perhaps one reason people did not intervene is that there is fear of being perceived as taking sides. There is widespread anti-French sentiment dating back to colonialism. A Chadian friend told me that I might have been better off just speaking English!

Another friend told me that my unrequited greeting of peace was a testament to those witnessing what happened. It made it clear that it was not a fight between two belligerent parties. It was a cultural insider attacking an outsider who was holding out his hand and speaking peace.

In the moment I felt completely powerless to change the situation. The only thing I could think to do was to keep offering goodwill, extending my hand, and the Islamic greeting of peace.

And then it hit me: how many times have Chadians extended peace to me, a stranger among them, with no reservation? They are experts at moving from *their* pain to *the* pain. When it comes down to it, most of us are--it's what it means to be a human in community. We bear each others' burdens--sometimes with grace, sometimes not.

That day I took an extra share of the burden. And I brought it to Jesus, who surely bears our grief and carries our sorrows.

But I felt some of my idealism die that day. What do you do when the peace you hope is possible seems suddenly so far away? When Christians and Muslims, on top of the religious separation we experience, are caught up in global political and cultural struggles? Is despair inevitable?

I decided to turn to an unlikely person: my local imam.

Meeting Isa

After more than two years in N'Djamena, Chad, I'd crossed paths with many of the men who live and work in front of the hospital where we live.

But I had yet to meet the imam of the largest mosque in the neighborhood. The angry confrontation at the peaceful cohabitation event showed me that I needed an ally. If a similar incident happened in our neighborhood, it might be more than I could bear. If I was to continue in Chad, something had to change.

So on a Friday morning I breathed a prayer and stepped out to try to make contact.

The first people I saw were some shopkeepers whom I greet regularly. I said to them, "I'd like to meet the imam. How can I do this?"

The shopkeepers pointed me down the street to a man doing laundry. His name was Toom ("Twin"). Toom referred me to a nearby group of men on motorbikes.

The moto-taxi drivers called over to a boy named Abdullahi. "Take him to see Sheikh Musa," they told him.

I followed Abdullahi through the neighborhood to a small prayer room beside the large mosque. There a young man named Musa looked up from his copy of the Qur'an. I told him I was also Abu Musa (our firstborn Moses goes by Musa in Chad).

"Are you the imam here?" I asked.

"Yes," he replied, "but not the big imam."

Musa called out to an older gentleman named Osman who was passing by.

Osman told me to wait under a tree, and stepped into a house nearby. He soon emerged with a bearded man who introduced himself as Sheikh Isa.

"Assalaam aleikum," I said to Imam Isa. "I am your neighbor, and also a person of faith. I thought that we should meet."

Isa invited me through the tin gate and pulled aside a curtain in his doorway. We sat on a carpet beside a small stack of Qur'ans. I said, "We both worship God, and I think God wants us to know each other."

Isa heartily agreed, and immediately began describing what the Qur'an says about Jesus (Isa). For ten minutes he talked about how Jesus had no earthly biological father, and how he declared himself blessed on the day of his birth, the day of his death, and the day of his resurrection (Qur'an 19:33). We were briefly interrupted by his wife bringing us biscuits and water.

Imam Isa described his activities of teaching children, leading prayers, and other responsibilities in the neighborhood. He invited me back anytime.

It was remarkable. The only information Isa had on me was that I was a Christian who lived at the nearby hospital, who loved and respected Muslims. This was enough for him to focus positively on the person of Jesus and to open up his home to me.

I learned several lessons that day.

First of all, asking for help--even with something as simple as finding someone's home--opens doors.

The second is that relationships rarely form through direct contact. They happen in chains and networks. It's not *what* you know, but *who* you know--and *who* you know can form in a surprising sequence if we take small steps to reach out.

And third, the chain of people who led me to Imam Isa was as impactful as my new friendship with him. Several days after our first meeting I again encountered Osman on the street, who greeted me with an enthusiastic, "It's been a while! Where have you been?" Groups of shopkeepers and motorcyclists know that I was seeking out Imam Isa. Now when I walk in the neighborhood, people call out, "So, are you going to visit Imam Isa?"

"Inshaallah," I reply.

It was all going so well until it wasn't.

I walked through the market to the local tailor to order a *jalabiya* (robe). On the way home I stopped to chat with a few friends at a corner stand. Across the road is a big house, where men often sit under the shade of a tree. That day there were only two men sitting there. I didn't know either of them.

The Spirit prompted me--with an intensity that happens rarely for me--to cross the street and say hello. I didn't particularly want to. I had other things to do at home. But when the Spirit says do something, it's best to do it.

So I crossed the sand and introduced myself in Arabic. I told them we live at the hospital and that I teach in town. The younger of the two men responded in a friendly way and told me he was named Abakar. So I asked the older man his name.

He gave me a hard stare. "Why? What do you want?"

This was all in Arabic, but he suddenly said in French, *Sortez*! I started to say that since we are neighbors, I wanted to be friends. He interrupted me and said again *Get out of here*!, with an angry wave of his hand. The younger man said nothing.

I was crestfallen and could only walk away. My chest hurt. Suddenly I was right back in the angry confrontation from three months earlier. The healing I'd experienced in my friendship with Imam Isa was undone by a sharp scratch to the wound.

The experience of being told to leave the country by an angry stranger came flooding back. It had been receding in my mind, but now I felt it keenly once again--the feeling that we are regarded not just with curiosity but with hostility; that our family is not safe if we fall into the whims of certain actors in the neighborhood, even places that I frequent; that we can never be accepted as a part of the community, even as an oddity, but that we can only delude ourselves into thinking we are building friendships until something like this jerks us out of the delusion.

Just as sharply, the question burned in my mind: Had I misunderstood the Spirit? Or had the Spirit deliberately led me into a hostile situation? Which was worse – to not trust my own spiritual discernment, or to not trust the Spirit?

I went home and sat in my chair, my heart heavy. I asked God to teach me something--anything--from this.

What I heard in response was, *Blessed are those who are persecuted for the sake of right relationships, for theirs is the kingdom of heaven.* Those who are motivated by the desire to build love and trust, to correct relationships that are eroded or fractured--will be blessed. The response--friendship or hostility--does not change the blessing.

I continued to walk my regular route. But I always felt uneasy passing by the big house near the market. Then one day I stopped to greet my friend Muhammad at the corner shop. We had first met through my quest to know Imam Isa. I turned to greet the others who were there.

I froze. Standing beside Muhammad was the very man who had dismissed me so rudely. My heart skipped a beat--was he about to sabotage my other friendships in the neighborhood? To turn people against me, and plant doubt in their hearts about whether I should be welcomed?

To my surprise, he extended his hand and greeted me warmly. What a difference it made to be treated as a friend by Muhammad!

On my way home I breathed a prayer--I'm sorry I doubted you, Spirit. You know what you're doing.

Every time I am met with hostility in a context where I feel vulnerable--where my family's safety is uncertain, or there is a risk of being expelled, or forces I don't understand drive the response of people to us--I'm reminded of the power of my own fear. Fear makes us think that making a mistake is the worst that could happen. But mission as guesting is messy. There is no such thing as doing mission without mistakes. To let the fear of doing it wrong paralyze us is to assume that one can get it right in the first place--which is simply not possible.

Jesus has incredible patience for his followers' small acts of faith, motivated by even the tiniest kernel of trust in him. Opening ourselves up to pain is the paradox of the Beatitudes--it turns out to be the only path to the kind of compassionate happiness that is intertwined with the happiness of others.[1]

So fear can paralyze. But it can also do something more insidious--it can take away hope. When I am mistreated as a foreigner, in my attempts to work for peace, it feels like something dies inside me. What is it--hope? Idealism? I used to think there was a difference. Now I'm not so sure.

Idealism is not the enemy; cynicism is. The worst attitude I can bring to my Muslim neighbor is not hostility or judgment, but the assumption that I know exactly how they'll respond to me. Calling it realism makes it no less insulting to imply that people are so one-dimensional that you can predict their responses.

Hope can actually be killed. Mine was, several times. But the remarkable quality of hope is that it resurrects. I brought the corpse of my idealism to Christ, and surrendered every aspect of my identity to him. He brought my hope to life again, with a guarantee of the future when the servant king will redeem the world.

Death and resurrection is the counterintuitive lesson of pain. Most religions have the idea that dying to self or to the world leads to new life. Suffering--that is, surrendering control--is what it takes to undermine our arrogance and our ignorance.[2]

I go back to the question posed to us after we were expelled from Somaliland--*what did you expect?* My answer is emphatically--I expected better! I did and do expect better from Muslim people. I expect them to be kind, hospitable, delightful neighbors. And most of the time I'm not disappointed.

I refuse to give up hope.

Jesus in Iran
"You are here because God sent you."

This was not what I expected to hear when I arrived in Iran. One of my hosts, Muhammad, sat me down and asked me point-blank why I had come. Having just passed through the harrowing process of getting a visa, I started to sweat a little bit.

I replied, "I'm not sure--I think the Holy Spirit led me here."

Muhammad nodded. "Last week I was so depressed I could barely move. I began to ask God for hope. Then I got the phone call that you were coming here for a conference. I found one of your sermons about Jesus online, and I thought, 'This is an answer to my prayers.' So that's why you are here."

I had to go to Iran to figure out why I was going to Iran.

It seems backwards, in a world where caution is a virtue. But there is a kind of knowledge that only comes with stepping out in faith.

I'm glad Muhammad could tell me why I was in Iran, because I was wondering it myself.

Sure, I knew *why* I was there--I'd been invited by an Islamic institute to participate in an interfaith dialogue through friends at my alma mater, Eastern Mennonite University.

And I knew *how* I got there--flying to Turkey to get a visa at the Iranian consulate in Istanbul, after months of waiting for approval from the Iranian government.

But the *meaning* of my trip was not entirely clear. Muhammad cleared it up for me. *You are here because God sent you.* And that's the sort of thing God does.

I went to Iran with fear and trembling. The US State Department labels Iran a *Do not travel: Level 4* country, "due to the risk of terrorism, civil unrest, kidnapping, arbitrary arrest of U.S. citizens, and wrongful detention." I was on my own--no one was going to come rescue me if something went wrong.

I chose to trust my Iranian hosts, as had other guests before me. But I still felt trepidation, and wondered how openly I could share my faith in Jesus. Would I risk confrontation or ridicule? Would I feel constrained by anxiety with every interaction?

To my surprise, I found myself speaking more candidly about my faith than I had any other place in the world. And I mean anywhere--I've preached and taught in lots of different contexts, and in Iran I shared my testimony at a more personal level than I ever had before. It's like I found language for my faith that was waiting to be unlocked.

What on earth was going on?

What I was experiencing was the exhilarating concoction of uncertainty and confidence that comes from being a religious guest, a misunderstood minority, a stranger in a strange land. There was an American Latter-day Saints scholar, me, and the rest were Shia Muslims.

I spent a lot of time crafting my presentations, carefully thinking about how I was going to represent Jesus in a way that was sensitive and compelling and true.

The conference in Qom, a center of Shia theology and religion, was called "Positive Global Ethics." So far so good. A nice tone, and a room full of friendly Shia clerics.

Other papers were presented in Farsi, with English interpretation. Then I read my carefully prepared paper on the biblical calling to be peacemakers. I gave special attention to the Sermon on the Mount.

After I finished, I learned that my paper was the only one for which a formal response had been prepared in advance. Since I was speaking about Jesus directly from the Bible at an Islamic academy, a professor at the academy was assigned to comment on what could be affirmed about my paper: Jesus' approach to peacemaking is creative, focused on reconciliation, deliverance from the cycle of revenge, and centered on service rather than power.

The professor then highlighted some points of ambiguity for a Muslim audience: How do you deal with the contradiction between the Hebrew Bible and the New Testament on killing? What would God's commandment to make war look like in our world? Since Jesus did not address war, could it be that peace for him is mostly *personal*?

Another presenter raised the practical question of a nonviolent response to the crisis in Gaza. I came to expect that question everywhere I went in Iran, and did my best to answer it.

It all went well. So why did I feel disappointed?

I came prepared for the big round table full of Shia clerics. It was as you might expect: dry discussion predicated on the philosophy that all we need is a little respect.

What I was *not* prepared for was how little of my actual witness happened in the context of the official meetings. I have no idea if something I said in those sessions did anything to make anyone think in a new way about Jesus. I actually doubt it.

What *did* provoke a response was when I shared from my personal journey. I had no intention of doing this--in fact, it was forced on me. After the planned meetings, my host told me that we were about to address a gathering of university students. About what? I asked. Oh, just talk about peacemaking, he said.

We were led to the stage of an auditorium full of students. I felt a moment of panic. I closed my eyes, took a deep breath, and asked the Holy Spirit for help.

A clear voice in my head replied, Just tell them who led you to Chad.

So I did. I told them how I obeyed the voice of *Isa al-Masih* (Jesus the Messiah) to work for peace between Christians and Muslims. I shared about the recent multi-faith meetings in central Chad, and the passages of the Qur'an and the Bible that participants cited as a motivation for building peace. The more we can create the kind of spaces where we share what is beautiful about our own faith and build trust, I suggested, the more the Holy Spirit can guide us into peace.

What a contrast to the dry and academic response of the clerics! The reaction of the students to a personal testimony was overwhelmingly positive. My host told me later that one woman was asking her friends, "Did he actually meet Isa al-Masih?"

Something shifted in that meeting. I opened myself up to just being a disciple of Jesus, speaking boldly of the simple beauty of the Jesus way. The question of how I ended up in Chad came up over and over, in the informal gatherings and the one-on-one conversations. I always responded, God called me. And when God invites you to do something, what do we do? We do it! My new Muslim friends all agreed.

One man in particular, Shaheed, wanted to have long conversations about it, as we were walking around the city and over tea. This idea that one could have a living relationship with God, listening to his voice, asking him for guidance, knocking on that door--this was compelling. It was far more interesting than comparing religions or making declarations or clever distinctions about what we believe.

I told Shaheed quite frankly: Sometimes I don't know why God has my family in Chad. But I have deep joy because we heard his voice in our hearts and we feel his presence. And that's enough.

Shaheed was stirred. You can have that kind of relationship with God? You can actually come to God as a friend? I saw in Shaheed a hunger for a sign that God is near to us--and that we can look for miracles of healing and reconciliation because we believe that God is active and present in our lives.

In Iran I was confronted with another aspect of the question *Why are you here?* Why would Shia Muslims and Mennonite Christians in particular strike up an unlikely friendship?

As we visited the holy sites of Shia Islam, the answer became obvious. Both communities draw an explicit connection between suffering and true faith. The stories of martyrdom are alive and well, centuries later.

Mennonites have the book *Martyrs Mirror*; Shia Muslims have the Battle of Karbala. My Iranian host wept openly as we stood before a painting of the murder of the infant Ali al-Asghar, held in the arms of his grieving father Imam Hussein. The bloodshed happened as Hussein was attempting to make peace with his enemies, and brought his young family along with him to show his good faith.

For Shia Muslims, Ali al-Asghar is the archetypal symbol of the innocent victim. They also hold up Hussein's father Imam Ali as a master peacemaker. His response to a polytheist enemy resonates with the gentleness and forgiveness of Jesus.

I met with several influential Ayatollahs (high-ranking clergy). One long-bearded Ayatollah with a twinkle in his eye opened his mouth and stories of peacemaking spilled out. He told me of Imam Ali doing all he could to avert war, and guarding the rights of his enemies. In another story, God asks the Prophet Musa why he didn't save Pharaoh from drowning in the Red Sea when he had the chance; God tells Musa that he created and loves even Pharaoh. The Ayatollah said that compassion is more important than rules; it is better to give away the last drops of water to a thirsty dog or to a parched plant than to do ablutions before prayer.

In response, I told the Ayatollah the story of Dirk Willems rescuing his pursuer, at great personal cost. He listened intently, and blessed me as we departed with a warm kiss on the cheek.

I later learned that this same Ayatollah is a staunch defender--often at odds with the regime--of Iran's religious minority communities: Christians, Zoroastrians, Baha'i, and Jews. It is not surprising that a Muslim of his quality sees the connection between the health of a society and the defense of its peace cells.

I was unprepared for how much I encountered Jesus in Iran.

Jesus Christ is held in high esteem, with references to him and his mother in the mosques, shrines, and popular piety. As I entered the home of one of my hosts, a respected Ayatollah, he pointed out a wall hanging that reads, "O Jesus of humanity, be in laughter, and revive humanity again." We shared an elaborate Persian feast under that banner, and I imagined the laughter of Jesus joining in with ours.

The celebrated Iranian poet Hafez said: "Jesus Christ is like glorious news of one coming, whose breath gives life to society."

I spoke very little in Iran about Christian doctrine, which is far less interesting than the day-to-day questions, challenges, and joys of Christian discipleship. My hope is for Iranians to encounter Jesus Christ--who already lives in Iran--in a way that is so intriguing and personal that they want to go deeper. It is through ordinary acts of discipleship that the glorious news of Jesus comes to any society, and breathes life into it.

I met Jesus in Iran. Not just that his name is scattered across the land in Persian script--in mosques, homes, and schools--but that he is actively breathing life into its society, laughing with joy as he comes. And it's good news.

It was good news for me too. When I spoke his name to Iranian friends as the one I love so much I would follow him anywhere, he breathed new life into me.

Jesus walks the edges of Iran. But that's exactly where you find him--in any society.

NOTES

[1]Andrew DeCort, *Blessed are the Others: Jesus' Way in a Violent World* (Middletown, DE: BitterSweetBooks, 2024), 11.
[2]Craig Greenfield, *Subversive Jesus: An Adventure in Justice, Mercy, and Faithfulness in a Broken World* (Grand Rapids MI: Zondervan, 2016), 154.

CHAPTER 4

A Stranger Faith

On my way home from teaching in Somaliland one day, I stopped at a shop to buy some produce. A Somali friend was with me. I entered with the ubiquitous greeting, *Assalaam aleikum* (peace be with you).

The shopkeeper turned to my friend and asked, "Is he a Muslim?"

"No," my friend replied.

"Then I won't greet him with the Islamic greeting," responded the shopkeeper.

I was surprised. I had been warmly welcomed by many different strangers in Somaliland. Yet someone had told this shopkeeper that religious boundaries are so important that they cannot be compromised, even with something as simple as a standard greeting. Religious identity shapes all aspects of our lives, to the point of dehumanizing each other.

In a situation like this I can't escape the problem of identity. Who am I?

Religious minorities know what it's like to be asked the inevitable: Why doesn't your faith match that of everyone else around here? I've been asked countless times in majority-Muslim contexts: Are you Muslim? (The inquiry is almost never posed to me in the West.)

Identity is a complicated and sometimes painful question. But it is basic to Christian discipleship. It's asking: How has my identity been disrupted, restored, and shaped by the one I have chosen to follow?

The world is divided into many kinds of *us* and *them*. What do we do with this crisis of identity? We have been taught that there are three options.[1]

The first is an *ethic for all*, consisting of Enlightenment values. In this view we are rational beings with access to universal principles of morality (we just have to figure out what those principles are).

Another option is finding *values in a closed community*. This approach assumes a sectarian group, in full control of its communal practices and without the responsibility of providing an ethic for everyone.

A third option is the post-modern version--finding our identity through liberation and individuality. Just figure out who *you* are as a person, and you'll be a fully-formed human being.

Each of these three options has some value, and contains some truth. But each is in tension with the heart of Christian faith: the abandonment of the self for the sake of love--a love that culminates in the scandal of the cross. We are not just autonomous beings. Nor are we strictly rational creatures who get our act together by discovering a universal set of rules. Neither can we seclude ourselves from the world--we share a planet brimming with neighbors to whom we have responsibility and a calling to love.

What if there is a fourth option, one rooted in Christian faith and the biblical story? What if we only find our true identity by *becoming the guest of others--becoming strangers for the sake of the gospel?*

At the core of Christian faith is a change of loyalty--the formation of an identity that we do not create but are given as a gift. The solution to division is not *oneness*; we need both difference from one another and a sense of belonging. The new identity we find in Christ is not that we become *self-less* (people lacking identity), but that we become *self-giving*, with an identity centered on creating space to receive the other.[2]

When a Muslim asks me *What religion are you?*, there's no stock answer. In some cases, I will answer directly that I am a Christian. In other cases it would be more confusing to apply a religious label without asking what presuppositions are behind it. What do you mean by Christian?

I choose to see it not as a threatening or complicated challenge, but as asking a more profound question: What do you think of *me* as a Muslim? Do you respect and love me?

What a gift to be asked by Muslims, directly and honestly, the very question I am hoping to answer--the reason I am there in the first place! They are asking, *Am I loved?*

So in almost every case, my immediate and first answer is--I love Muslims. It helps that this is a simple statement to make in any language. But more importantly, it establishes an attitude that shapes the whole conversation that follows.

The reason that God calls us to become strangers is to give us concrete opportunities to answer the world's deepest identity question: *Do you love us?*

A stranger faith is one that moves into the neighborhood. It says *yes* to the religious other. It translates God's welcome into the language of the world.

A stranger faith is also just that: peculiar. It is not normal or expected to seek vulnerability. But the more vulnerable we become, the more clearly we represent the nonviolent, transformative gospel of Jesus Christ.

Mission as becoming strangers

Is showing up in a strange land just a side effect of mission? Or is it essential to what mission means?

Consider the spiritual ancestors of all Christians, Muslims, and Jews. The community of faith in Scripture begins with God's calling to Abram and Sarai to leave their homes and become guests in another land. The pilgrim family was required to trust in God's goodness and guidance, not because they were at the center of power but because God had called them to *go*.[3]

The entry into the promised land was delayed, which teaches an important lesson: We do not need a specific geographic location to live in faithfulness to God. It is possible to be God's people without a territorial claim. In fact, there are far more important things than entering the land.[4]

After the disastrous experiment with state power, God's people once again found themselves as pilgrims, this time in forced exile. They had to learn to live again as strangers in a strange land. The exile serves as a reminder that Israel's God is not like other gods, who are bound by nation or territory.

Good guesting abounds in the Hebrew Bible. Daniel prayed for Babylon, which both showed his concern for his exiled home--and also declared that God was bigger than Babylon's mighty empire.

Jeremiah 29:7 gives us the beautiful passage that is a paradigm of good guesting: seek the peace of the city to which God has summoned you--in other words, its welfare in the long haul.

Elijah, Daniel, and Obadiah all give us examples of *service* as fundamental to good guestwork, out of obedience to God.[5]

So the Hebrew Bible, especially the parts that Jesus explicitly identified with, expresses faithfulness to God in terms of being strangers that bless the world. This is Jesus' tradition. Jesus engaged constantly in guestwork, especially because he had no home as such (Matt 8:20). The closest thing to a home that he had was a town where people were strenuously opposed to him (Luke 4:16-30). It is precisely in his role as a guest that Jesus proclaims the hospitality of God.[6]

Jesus demands a life full of works of mercy, most poignantly in the parable of the sheep and the goats. But it is curious that he rarely practiced mercy in the role of a *host*. We do not read stories of Jesus clothing the naked, visiting the prisoner, or sheltering the homeless. We read about one instance of Jesus feeding the hungry.

In contrast, Jesus' most transformative exchanges happened when he was the *guest*, not the host. Consider Jesus' forays into people's homes. Matthew the tax collector invites Jesus to dinner. He is welcomed by

Martha and Mary (Luke 10:38), Simon the Leper (Matt 26:6-7), a Pharisee (Luke 7:36), a leader of the Pharisees to celebrate Sabbath (Luke 14:1), and to a wedding (John 2:2). The Samaritan woman draws water for him. The disciples on the road to Emmaus do not recognize the resurrected Christ until they welcome Jesus as a stranger to a shared meal. Before Jesus sends out the seventy-two disciples, he makes them dependent on hospitality by stripping them of their resources. For Jesus, *being* strangers ourselves seems to be as important as welcoming them.[7]

In some cases, Jesus himself presses for an invitation. Jesus recognizes that becoming a guest, even forcefully so, breaks down barriers that prevented others from seeing who we was. He chooses to become dependent on someone who is alienated from his own community, Zacchaeus the despised tax collector. Everyone's eyes are opened--Zacchaeus, the disciples, and onlookers who criticize Jesus for becoming a guest in the home of a sinner.[8]

At a certain level Jesus violates norms of hospitality, making his hosts very uncomfortable.[9] Much of what the Gospels record about Jesus as a guest is also paired with the response of his critics. When the Pharisees see him eating with tax collectors and sinners, they grumble that he is a guest where he should not be (Luke 19:7). In the cases where he accepts invitations from Pharisees, he is being watched closely and suspiciously. He disturbs his host in Luke 7 by his response to a woman who anoints his feet with her hair. Jesus says that her sins are forgiven as a result of her actions of hospitality, as a guest in a hostile environment!

The meal scenes in Luke are Jesus' speech acts that call religious leaders to repent and share fellowship with "sinners," extending the inclusive hospitality of the kingdom to women, children, slaves, the sick, and the marginalized.[10] The parable he tells of the great banquet recognizes that in the eternal kingdom those who are poor now will inherit imperishable homes. Then they will have a chance to repay the welcome they received in the previous life.[11]

Good guestwork is for everyone, poor and rich alike. Downward mobility--entering into the reality of the marginalized--is an integral part of the gospel. But it is only half of the dynamic described throughout Scripture. Mary articulates it in her song: "He has brought down the powerful from their thrones...and lifted up the lowly" (Luke 1:52). These two dynamics, bringing down and lifting up, are both aspects of Jesus' guestwork. We see Jesus becoming a guest of both the powerful religious leaders and wealthy elites of his society, as well as the marginalized.

With the amount of guestwork that Jesus engages in, it is not surprising that he thinks and teaches about how to do it well. He urges his hearers to take the lowly seat, rather than the seat of honor (Luke 14:7-23). He sends out his followers as vulnerable guests who say words of peace in whatever house they enter, and who eat whatever is put before them (Luke 10).

Jesus places immense value on table fellowship, on being both guests and hosts, on visiting and being visited. Jesus' words in Revelation are both spiritual and material: "Behold, I stand at the door and knock; if anyone hears my voice and opens the door, I will come in to them and will dine with them, and they with me" (Rev 3:20). He calls himself the universal guest, so that we are meant to see Jesus in every stranger at our door: "I was a stranger, and you did (or did not) invite me in; naked, and you did (or did not) clothe me; sick, and in prison, and you did (or did not) visit me" (Matt 25:31-46).

When Jesus calls us to follow him, therefore, we are called into both dimensions of hospitality: both welcoming strangers and *becoming* strangers who knock on doors, seeking shelter, warmth, and relationship.

In what follows, we will consider three characteristics of a stranger faith--both in the sense of being guests and of being peculiar.

Strangers find roots in Christ away from powerful centers

Christians sometimes worry that too much contact with Muslims will erode one's faith. I've often heard Christians, even those who are making the argument for reaching out to Muslims, advise others to be spiritually cautious when meeting Muslims. Prepare your heart through prayer, arm yourself with the Word of God, and be on guard.

Very good advice--and in keeping with Jesus' admonition to be alert (Mark 13:9).

But the implication of this approach is that the closer you get to Muslims, the more spiritual danger you face.

What this overlooks is the dangers of *not* becoming guests – the dangers of security, complacency, comfort, and wealth. These were the warnings Jesus issued. Not once did he say, Be on guard for what friendship with Samaritans will do to your faith. What did he tell the disciples to watch out for? The teachings of the leaders in their own religious tradition (Matt 16).

On the contrary--it is dangerous for Christians to *avoid* Muslims. We fall prey to all kinds of temptations when we attempt to separate ourselves. The traps of wealth and security are powerful, especially because we usually aren't able to see them until we step out as vulnerable guests.

We tend to assume that seeking the comfort of a powerful center--the places where people who share our culture and faith are in charge--is spiritually healthy. But the truth is actually the opposite. It is the testing of our faith that happens when we become religious minorities that shapes us into the image of Christ.

By becoming strangers, immersed in a world of another religion, we move deeper into our own faith commitments. Some of the most profound Christian reflections come from followers of Christ living in environments that seem contradictory to who Jesus is.[12] Paradoxically, this is where Jesus is often revealed most clearly.

One example is Father Louis Massignon, who turned to faith in Christ through his time spent with Muslims in North Africa. Massignon wrote, "I had become, through the apprenticeship of Arabic, the liturgical language of Islam...converted to Christianity by the witness to God implied by the Muslim faith."[13]

Another example is the Christian missionary-monk Charles de Foucauld (d. 1916), who lived for many years among Tuareg Muslims in

North Africa. After observing his life carefully, a Muslim writer named Ali Merad remarked that de Foucauld found true happiness in imitating Jesus--and in treating each person he met as if he were encountering Jesus. Merad concludes that this mode of imitating and seeing Jesus is, from the perspective of Muslims, the most powerful way to espouse the authenticity of the gospel message.[14] When Muslims tell us what draws them to Jesus--we should pay attention!

What is the key to bearing authentic witness to Jesus among Muslims? It is taking the good news of Jesus outside the gates of power, outside the cultural and religious centers that distort his message and his person.

The story of Babel in Genesis 11 lays some important groundwork for mission. The contrast is clear between the enforced uniformity of empire on the one hand-- and on the other, Abram's calling to *go*. Christian faith was never meant to have a center. Humans are drawn to homogeneity, but God loves diversity.

This means that mission should always be centrifugal--moving outward---rather than centripetal--pulling inward. This is not to ignore issues of power; in fact, just the opposite. As long as there are powerful and powerless, mission is best expressed not by expecting the powerless to *come*, but by the powerful *going*--and in so doing relinquishing some influence and privilege.[15]

One of the fundamental expressions of Christian faith is that God gives the chance for the powerful to become powerless for the sake of relationships. Those who presume that they are hosts--due to a dominant language, culture, military, border policy, longevity in a place, or whatever form Babel takes--are given the gift of being scattered by a God who cares about both the powerful and the powerless.

What we learn from the empire-building of Babel, and in contrast from the obedience of Abram and Sarai, is that God seeks to deliver us from the trappings of presumed hosting. Learning a non-dominant language is deliverance.[16] Serving in a context where one gives up majority status, cultural dominance, or territorial ownership is deliverance too.

Mission is about being good guests because God is delivering all of us from empire and into something more beautiful--the kingdom of Jesus.

The recognition that the Christian condition is that we are perpetually guests of God and others is the antidote to the Christendom mentality that we should run the world. It is the difference between a strategy and a tactic; a strategy identifies a place that is its own, from which exterior threats are managed. But tactics are taken in the space of the other. The church is not a strategy; it is always in exile in a world full of domination.[17]

Rather than extending our sense of territory into our mission context, as the Christendom model tempts us to do, good guestwork challenges the very notion of territorialism and turns our attention to the margins. The reality is that Christian hospitality is most vibrantly practiced at the margins, because people who have a sense of their own alien status are able to blur the lines between guest and host.[18]

Blurring the lines is a threatening prospect for powerful centers. A Christendom mentality finds unexpected identity markers confusing; you are either in or out, us or them, for or against our project. But at the margins of empire there is grace for difference.

Strangers say yes

A friend named Muktar called to invite me to a Somali wedding in Djibouti. I was tired from a day of teaching, and I knew that it would go late into the night. So I respectfully declined.

"It's too bad," he said as we hung up. "You would learn a lot about Somali culture from this."

What a gift he was offering--and I didn't have the strength to accept.

But I learned my lesson. The next time Muktar called me up, I said yes.

He took me to a small makeshift cinema to watch a soccer game. Muktar elbowed us up to the front, near the screen, and was soon confronted loudly. "I'll be right back," he told me, and stepped outside.

When he came back inside a few minutes later, he was disheveled and dirty. One eye was slightly puffy. When I asked him what happened, he explained that he just had to fight a few guys to get me a prime seat.

Unexpected things happen when we say yes. In this case, saying yes to Muktar meant making my first real friend in Djibouti--one who would even fight for me.

When Christian presence is freed from the confines of power, it offers a radical *yes* to the host culture--not just to individual invitations, but demonstrating a posture of openness and embrace.

The more that Christians can become guests of Muslim neighbors, or people of any other or no faith, the more space we open up for understanding and seeing God at work, for us and for them. Virginia Cobb, a pioneer of respectful witness among Muslims, states that our attitude should inspire confidence in "our sincere desire to serve them, our fair-mindedness, sensitivity and appreciation for all that is good. We should emphasize every point of agreement, encourage every true direction, praise all that is praise-worthy, put the best possible interpretation on every teaching or practice."[19]

This is what a radical *yes* means as a guest--putting the best possible light on what we observe in our hosts. Saying yes has practical implications for language, diet and fasting habits, schedule, dress, and many other questions.

But does it go further? Does the yes extend even to the explicitly *religious* practices of our Muslim neighbors, like praying in the mosque, or reading the Qur'an and the Hadith?

For Muslims, the life of faith is tied up intricately with cultural practices. It is next to impossible, therefore, to compartmentalize our guest-work. In other words, as guests of Muslims we cannot show cultural and social respect without also demonstrating respect for religious practices.

The discipline of putting the best possible interpretation on every teaching or practice turns out to be the most important way to bear witness to Jesus. Strangers develop these skills of saying yes in ways that others do not. When the Christendom mentality of a central power gives way to a stranger posture, we begin to view the interfaith encounter in terms of an exchange of gifts. If my neighbor of another faith has some-thing to offer me, I must be open to change if I truly enter the vulnera-ble state that guesting demands.[20]

Open to change? That sounds like losing your faith. But that's not what I mean at all.

Becoming a stranger does *not* mean that one's faith is absorbed into the majority faith of the host culture. If anything, the opposite is the case; those who assume that the way in which faith is preserved is by em-bedding it in structures of power run the greater risk of their faith being swept up in the ideologies of empire: militarism, racism, and greed.

In contrast, seeing interfaith hospitality as an exchange of gifts places faith where it belongs--at the margins of power.

At a seminary in France, I suggested that Muslims and Christians see each other as allies in the quest for peace. One student raised her finger and asked, "Doesn't this just mean sweeping our differences under the rug?"

I was grateful that she raised this important question. Sharing gifts does *not* mean creating a sort of synthesis. On the contrary! The differ-ences often become even clearer in the process of the exchange.

A good example is the dialogue, now translated into more than a dozen global languages, co-written by a Muslim named Badru Kateregga and a Christian named David Shenk.[21] As guests, we often find ourselves more willing and able to articulate our faith than when we move in spaces where a version of our faith is assumed.

Good guestwork means that *the basic mode of Christians should be to say yes to offers of interfaith hospitality*. What I mean is that we should not be surprised when our neighbors of other faiths reach out to us with gestures of friendship and invitation. And our response should be to ac-cept as often as possible. When Muktar offers to take you to a wedding or to the football match, *say yes*.

But here's the tricky part, where the rubber meets the road: What about the basic invitation to conversion? Christians living among a

Muslim majority know that such commendations are common, even from strangers (as do Muslims living among Christian majorities). I have received countless admonitions to embrace Islam.

Clearly we cannot simply convert upon invitation. Allegiance to Jesus allows for nothing that will stand in the way of following him.

Yet there are ways to respond to these kinds of pressures that do not involve changing religious affiliation, ways that build peace and mutual attachment and that help us grow as disciples who are at home as strangers.

What I mean is this--when our Muslim neighbors invite us to convert it is usually accompanied by other sorts of callings. Some of these invitations a committed Christian can readily accept: to read the Qur'an, to understand Islam more fully, even to taste some of the goodness and benefits of practices like communal prayers, fasting, charity, cleanliness, decency, and a host of other moral norms. Even in the call to conversion we can ask: What can we say *yes* to here?

To our neighbors In the Muslim society where we've lived, we generally present our identity not first as Christian (which carries negative connotations for many Muslims) but as People of the Book (*Ahl al-Kitab* in Islam).

So our neighbors know we are not Muslims, but neither do we easily fit into the religious categories. As guests, it is important for us to adapt to the culture of our neighborhood. Christy wears a veil and I wear Islamic garments, and we use Islamic religious language. When we moved into a busy urban neighborhood in Zanzibar, a friendly neighbor gave me an Islamic name that is easier for others to pronounce and remember.

About a year into living in that neighborhood, I started to receive invitations to pray in the local mosque. The mosque is a center of both religious and social life. You are not truly a part of the neighborhood unless you participate there.

So it made sense after living there for a while, walking the streets with our children, drinking tea, and making known that we were people of faith, that friends invited me to join them in the social and religious gathering of *salat* (prayer). I had received and accepted this sort of invitation in other places, and had been tutored in the prayer forms by Muslim friends. So I knew what to expect.

What I didn't anticipate was how much deeper my relationships became as a result of that decision. To pray alongside the same people from whom I buy fruit and with whom I drink tea--it was transformative. I did not impose myself, but said yes to an invitation. I never stopped being a stranger--but I felt closer to Jesus in the mosque than I did anywhere else in Zanzibar.

A Christendom mentality would struggle to understand how powerful it is to be a religious guest. Praying in the mosque along with my friends opened up doors for witness to Jesus that I'd never had before.

Perhaps a time will come when I can reciprocate the invitation. I hope that my Muslim friends receive the same warm hospitality when they cross the threshold of a church building.

Strangers translate

"Are you trying to convert people on their own turf?"

This was the question posed to me by a college friend as I explained to him why I was going to East Africa with a service organization. His question was meant to challenge me, and it worked. He was confronting me with all the messaging that I had been receiving in academic environments--messages fraught with anxiety about mission shaped by postcolonialism and skepticism.

Looking back, I am grateful for his direct question. Too often these worries are simply left unstated, and we all miss out on some great conversation about mission.

Rabindranath Tagore, the Nobel-Prize-winning Bengali Indian poet, wrote that when Christians "bring their truth to a strange land, unless they bring it in the form of homage it is not accepted and should not be."[22]

In response to the good question posed by my college friend, my simple answer is that I want my presence among Muslims to be received as homage. I am not the bearer of a message that I must figure out how to make known in a strange land. I have no strategy. I have only tactics for finding ways to turn our attention together to Jesus, the matchless guest in our midst.

Strangers travel light. When Jesus sent out the seventy-two disciples, he instructed them to take nothing for the journey—no staff, no bag, no bread, no money, no extra shirt (Luke 9:3). They were meant to proclaim a kingdom marked by simplicity.

Converting people is too heavy a burden for anyone to bear. This is why Jesus releases us from anything but a simple proclamation of the kingdom. Travel light--leave your baggage behind.

Is the gospel like *cargo*? As strangers, we are freed from seeing the gospel as a set of beliefs or practices that we must drag across a cultural bridge. Treating the gospel as cargo reduces it to an object. As the Bengali poet observed, the result is that we are unable to understand or accept when something new is going on. We see what we expect to see--hearers either accepting or rejecting a message. We might miss the reality of hearers accepting the gospel in a way that we did not expect.

What is the problem with thinking of the gospel as cargo? First, the notion that God works only through a *message* is simply not the case. God is already present in any context where Christians arrive. Christendom's search for universalism turned Christianity into a set of beliefs.[23] But a mere message has no need of a Messiah. When contextualization becomes about reducing the gospel to a message, it subtly rejects the unsettling, counter-cultural way of Jesus.

Second, there is no essence of Christian faith, no single version of the gospel. That is to say, there is no Christian culture. In every case the gospel must be received as a cross-cultural--or better said counter-cultural--reality. Even the Western enlightenment project of asking the original meaning of the text for its hearers is impossible, because it is a quest for the single correct reading.[24]

There is no single correct reading of the Bible. And this is good news! It puts the hearer in a position of agency; it is not the missionary who brings a correct understanding of Scripture and seeks a contextual equivalent. The power imbalance between the missionary and the local hearer is challenged at its core. We all come to Jesus and to the Bible as strangers, hosted by the strange, convicting, and joyful world they offer us.

Does this mean that there is more than one gospel? Yes! Four, to be precise, in the New Testament alone. And many more in all kinds of different settings. The work of God in Christ is described in many ways.

So sharing the gospel does not consist of taking some form or set of practices of the Christian faith and putting this into some other setting. Instead, the Spirit moves people to respond to what the Scriptures claim about Christ.[25]

What we call emergent and insider movements are therefore the unique response of people in their own ways to Christ, not simply adapting some essential doctrines or practices into their own cultural context.

Mission is dialogue, not putting a fresh coat of paint on an old vehicle. It is relational, not recyclable.

Perhaps the most obvious limit to the *cargo* view of faith is with our own children. In Iran I was struck by the anxiety that Muslims and Christians share about how to transmit faith to the next generation.

But if we take an approach to mission as being strangers, we will not be taken aback when even our own children turn out to be strangers to us.[26] In meeting with religious leaders in Iran, I proposed that the first interfaith dialogue we have is with our children, whose experience of the world is different from our own. The same skills we need to meet the religious other, we use in sensitively sharing what is important to us about our faith with those in our care.

Heads were nodding in agreement around the room. Iranians are asking how to foster faith in their children, as are people of faith in the

West. Both societies perceive a crisis of faith--young people are losing their religion.

For certain people in the room, however, the answer was straightforward--we simply have to enforce the ethical standards we believe in, and the younger generation's faith will follow. Others shared with me later (in private) that this sort of denial of the generational change that is already happening is widespread in the older religious leadership.

We need a better approach for sharing our faith than the cargo image--the package of beliefs and practices that we unload on our neighbors or our children. Proclaiming the gospel to Muslims as strangers helps us proclaim the gospel to other strangers in our midst--our own children.

So what is the alternative to the *cargo* idea of the gospel as we face the challenge of adapting to diverse situations? West African theologian Lamin Sanneh offers an alternative: *translation*.

According to Sanneh, translation is the key to why Christian faith took root in many nonwestern cultures. Most Christian expansion occurred after colonialism and during the period of national awakening, in which colonialism was an obstacle to faith. Translating the Bible into African languages helped Africans view Christian faith in a positive light, and also fostered African agency in leadership, including younger people and women.

Western missionaries imagined that the stronger the indigenous religion, the more resistance there would be to the gospel. In fact, Africans responded most enthusiastically to Christian faith in the places where the indigenous religions were the strongest. Sanneh even identifies one simple factor indicating that the gospel would be well received: if people continued to use their indigenous name for God.[27]

In Uganda a massive billboard looms beside a highway, reading *Allah and God are NOT the same person.* Who could have spent the money to broadcast such a message? The minority Muslim community of Kampala? On closer inspection, I saw that the billboard was created by a church.

There are many reasons to affirm that Allah and the Christian God are the same being--perhaps the most basic being that Allah is simply the Arabic name for God, which Arab Christians have used for millennia, up till today.[28] But even aside from that, what an opportunity for Christians to build a bridge! Rather than feeling threatened by a different name for God, we should celebrate what Sanneh has recognized as the gift of translation--that God already has a name for Muslims.

Sanneh states that the end of Christendom came not with secularization, but with mother tongues as the means of receiving the gospel.[29] The New Testament is from its beginning a translated version of the message of Jesus, meaning that Christianity is a faith without a revealed language. It is unique in that it is transmitted apart from the language and culture of its founder.

In fact, so deeply embedded is the translation DNA that Christians tend to act as if their language is the original language of the Bible.[30] If any religion has the antidote to the poison of colonialism, cultural domination, and Christendom built into it from its very origins, Christianity is that faith.

I teach a course on the theology of Scripture at a Chadian evangelical seminary. In the course we consider the question: What does it mean to call the Bible the word of God?

The students' first response is usually to describe it as a divinely revealed document, with no mention of the human element. But when we read together how Muslim writers explain the revelation of the Qur'an, the students can readily spot the difference. The role of the Qur'an in the Islamic community is more equivalent to the role of Jesus (not the Bible) for Christians.

And one of the major differences between the received books is the attitude toward *language*. Because Christians have never viewed the Bible as Muslims view the Qur'an, the priority of different languages becomes so important to Christian faith. Languages have merit in themselves and in God's eyes.

Translation is the nonviolent option for spreading a faith. Bible translation is the exact opposite of forcing religion on people. The demands of language and professional study, the respect for local forms and usage--these are totally inconsistent with coercing people or trying to fix the outcome.[31]

What does translation have to do with mission as being strangers? Simply this: that the Word of God (Jesus) and the word of God (the Bible) both present themselves as *guests* of the beloved human beings they have come to save. Translation is another word for good guestwork. It sheds any sense of cultural or moral superiority in favor of a radical quest for relationship.

The *cargo* view of the gospel asks: How can I make the good news relatable or relevant for the other? What is the bare minimum of freight I need to bring across the cultural bridge, while getting rid of the non-essentials?

In contrast, translation asks: How can I learn to speak the language of the other so that we can help each other embrace the good news of Jesus Christ?

There is no substitute for becoming a guest of the other if the gospel is to be translated. No witness exists without some kind of moving into the neighborhood. Noel Castellanos writes, "Can you imagine Jesus commuting to Nazareth from heaven every day instead of being fully present in the everyday situations of his family and neighbors?"[32] What we do with our bodies matters, including where we spend our days, where we live and raise our children, and to whom we become neighbors.

In other words, we do not carry the message--we take part in the message.

And when we do that together--as part of what I call *peace cells*--amazing things happen.

NOTES

[1] Miroslav Volf, *Exclusion and Embrace* (Nashville: Abingdon, 1996), 20-26.

[2] Ibid., 40-58.

[3] Christopher J. H. Wright, *Old Testament Ethics for the People of God* (Downers Grove, Illinois: InterVarsity, 2004), 221-23.

[4] Ida Glaser, *The Bible and Other Faiths: Christian Responsibility in a World of Religions* (Downers Grove, IL: InterVarsity, 2005), 102.

[5] Wright, *Old Testament Ethics*, 240-43.

[6] Amos Yong, *Hospitality and the Other: Pentecost, Christian Practices, and the Neighbor* (Maryknoll, NY: Orbis, 2008), 101.

[7] Chico Fajardo-Heflin, "Waiting to be Welcomed: Learning to Be a Guest, Not a Giver," *Plough Quarterly* No. 6: Witness Profiles, November 4, 2015. Available at https://www.plough.com/en/topics/community/leadership/waiting-to-be-welcomed

[8] Paul-Gordon Chandler, *Pilgrims of Christ on the Muslim Road: Exploring a New Path between Two Faiths* (Lanham, MD: Rowman & Littlefield, 2007), 92.

[9] Robert J. Karris, *Eating Your Way Through Luke's Gospel* (Collegeville, MN: Liturgical, 2006), 44.

[10] Yong, *Hospitality and the Other,* 102.

[11] Derek W. Engdahl, *The Great Chasm: How to Stop Our Wealth from Separating Us from the Poor and God* (Pomona, CA: Servant Partners, 2015) Kindle edition, location 642.

[12] Chandler, *Pilgrims*, 96-97.

[13] Ibid., 97.

[14] Ali Merad, *Christian Hermit in an Islamic World: A Muslim's View of Charles de Foucauld* (New York: Paulist, 1999), 21. Cited in Chandler, *Pilgrims*, 129.

[15] Andy McCullough, *Global Humility: Attitudes for Mission* (Welwyn Garden City: Malcolm Down, 2018), Kindle edition, locations 1446-75.

[16] Deborah Bernhard and Marcus Grohmann, eds., *Vulnerable Mission for Practitioners* (Dresden: Alliance for Vulnerable Mission, 2025), 74.

[17] Stanley Hauerwas, *After Christendom: How the Church is to Behave if Freedom, Justice and a Christian Nation Are Bad Ideas* (Nashville: Abingdon, 1991), 16-18.

[18] Christine Pohl, *Making Room: Recovering Hospitality as a Christian Tradition* (Grand Rapids: MI. Wm B. Eerdmans Publishing Co., 1999), 6, 124.

[19] Virginia Cobb, "Methods for Work among Muslims" (paper given at the Teheran Conference, 1969). Cited in Chandler, *Pilgrims*, 98.

[20] Thomas Ogletree, *Hospitality to the Stranger: Dimensions of Moral Understanding* (Philadelphia: Fortress, 1985), 4.

[21] Badru Kateregga and David Shenk, *A Muslim and a Christian in Dialogue* (Scottdale, PA: Herald, 1997)

[22] E. Stanley Jones, *The Christ of the Indian Road* (London: Hodder & Stoughton, 1925), 23

[23] Hauerwas, *After Christendom*, 16.

[24] William A. Dyrness, *Insider Jesus: Theological Reflections on New Christian Movements* (Downers Grove, IL: InterVarsity, 2016), 20-21, 24.

[25] Ibid., 22.

[26] Mortimer Arias writes, "Every generation – inside or outside the church – has to be evangelized, that is, confronted with the good news of the kingdom of Jesus Christ. And every generation of Christians has the unique and nontransferable responsibility of sharing the good news with its own generation." Mortimer Arias, *Announcing the Reign of God: Evangelization and the Subversive Memory of Jesus* (Lima, OH: Academic Renewal, 2001), xi.

[27] Lamin Sanneh, *Whose Religion Is Christianity? The Gospel beyond the West* (Grand Rapids, MI: Wm. B. Eerdmans Publishing Co., 2003), 18.

[28] Miroslav Volf, *Allah: A Christian Response* (New York: Harper-One, 2011), 84.

[29] Sanneh uses the term Christendom in a somewhat different way from Anabaptists, who speak of Christendom as the ties between church and state in which all citizens are considered "Christian" by default. This is how Stuart Murray can argue that the fall of Christendom in the West is both something to grieve and also a hopeful and necessary development for faithful Christian discipleship. Stuart Murray, *The Naked Anabaptist: The Bare Essentials of a Radical Faith* (Harrisonburg, VA: Herald, 2012), 82.

[30] Sanneh, *Whose Religion is Christianity?*, 24, 97-98, 104.

[31] Ibid., 100, 113.

[32] Noel Castellanos, *Where the Cross Meets the Street: What Happens to the Neighborhood When God Is at the Center* (Downers Grove, IL: InterVarsity, 2015), Kindle edition, locations 1019-21.

CHAPTER 5

Peace Cells

In the film *Taken*, Liam Neeson warns kidnappers over the phone: *I have a very particular set of skills*. He is referring to his ability to track and defeat criminals.

Religious minorities also have a *particular set of skills*--the skills of resisting hostile majorities. Skills of surviving the waves of enmity that sweep through societies. Of reaching out across divides. Of forgiving.

How do they come by these skills? The same way one learns any-thing--by necessity.

Take language as an example. Language learning is hard. It is a long process, full of ups and downs. It makes a huge difference how you feel about your language skills. Seeing progress is tremendously motivating, and disappointment is deeply *de*-motivating.

But *you learn the language that you need*. It takes time, and you seem to never reach the point you hope, but the *necessity* of language for daily tasks is what motivates and sustains real learning.

So the task of learning a language is at least as much about what *cir-cumstances* you throw yourself into (or find yourself thrown into) as it is about the particulars of what you do to learn. Want to learn Viet-namese? Move to Vietnam. Trying to learn Spanish? Find a job where the customer base is Spanish-speaking. You will eventually obtain the language skills you need.

The same is true of peacemaking. Reaching out across lines of hostility is not simply a matter of learning tools, finding theological motivation, or even making contact with people who are different.

Just as important is experiencing at a deeply personal level the *need* for peacemaking. And who is in the best position to experience this need in an interfaith rivalry? Religious minorities--the people I call *peace cells*.

Color and fine detail

In a negative light, sometimes the biological image of *cells* is used to describe small, covert groups of individuals who are engaging in some kind of extremist behavior--gathering intelligence, acquiring weapons, and executing attacks.

But what I mean is the exact opposite effect of minority identity--the positive motivation, planning, and tactics for peacebuilding. Religious minorities act as *peace cells*, playing a unique role in their societies.

Peace cells, when you say it out loud, sounds like *P-cells*, which in the context of neuroscience are the cells that help us process color and fine details. The P is short for *parvus*, the Latin word for small. Religious minorities, in their insignificant numbers, play an outsized role in helping us see. They help us see *color*--the great value of difference, beauty, and contrast in our lives; and they help us see *fine detail*--the important factors, people, or relationships that majorities overlook.

In their most blatant and unapologetic forms, majorities are dangerous, devolving into a mob. But majorities can be just as dangerous when they are less obvious, seeking to create uniformity or erase difference. Majorities act in the name of security, defending the country from some political, cultural, or religious threat. This inevitably backfires; a society suffers when its minorities are silenced or defeated. Put positively, religious minorities offer something invaluable to a society: a drive for reconciliation.

These gains do not come without pain, however. Our children attend a French-language school in Chad. There are few Christian families at the school, and sometimes the other children make it clear that the Muslim majority does not understand Christian faith. A classmate asked our seven-year-old daughter, "Do you pray?" She said that yes, she does. He replied, "But you're American--you don't pray!" Evidently he meant praying in the mosque, or in Islamic style. Our daughter had no reply.

To be a religious minority is a difficult burden to bear in any context. Facing the challenging questions of assimilation, how to raise one's children, how openly to express one's faith, as well as uncertainty about how one's minority status affects legal questions, results in accumulating pressures that those in the majority simply do not have to address.

But the religious minority identity comes with certain advantages; by necessity one becomes an ally-seeker, which is another way to describe a peacemaker. So when we look for those whom Jesus calls the "children of God" (Matt 5:9), we are likely to find them among minority groups, who have learned through struggle to look for partners in the unlikeliest of places.

In short, peace cells form because the survival of minorities depends on alliances. In the process they take on a *new* identity--alongside other identity markers such as race, ethnicity, or religion--that of a bridge-builder. The identity of peacemaker does not displace other identities, but rather enriches them.

A different flavor

Palestinian pastor Munther Isaac left Palestine for a season for seminary education. As he was leaving, he was surprised when a Muslim friend in Ramallah told him that he must come back and do something about all of the young Christians leaving Palestine. We need you here, was the main message of this Muslim man to his Christian friend, and Isaac says, "He then went on naming off the different cultural and educational initiatives in Ramallah that were started or led by Christians! 'You bring a different taste to our society,' he said."[1]

What is that taste that minorities bring? For one, they upend what we think we know about weakness and disadvantage. Psychologist Hara

Estroff Marano was seated next to a business leader on a flight, who confided that "she now makes it a point *not* to hire any but the children of first-generation immigrants. Why? I asked. Because, she said, she has found that the kids of immigrant parents are resourceful, hardworking, and good at figuring things out and at problem solving....Their 'disadvantage' wound up making them stronger."[2] Religious minorities take apparent weaknesses--lack of power and influence, misunderstandings, and even persecution--and turn them into problem-solving strengths.

Being a minority requires the development of particular kinds of muscles. It takes practice to see oneself through another's eyes, and if we are not forced to do it we simply won't. Psychologists have studied the effect that feeling powerful has on our decision-making processes. Those who feel powerful trust their intuition; they do not feel the need to question whether someone else's experience or view should shape theirs.[3]

In other words, the powerful have little chance to practice what Miroslav Volf calls "double vision"--recognizing the other's sense of justice or injustice, the other's experience and point of view. This practice is fundamental to becoming willing to *embrace* the other, to overcome the exclusionary us and them and to seek reconciliation.[4]

Peace cells have a *very particular set of skills*.

They look for *space* wherever they can find it.

They engage in *tactics* to build bridges.

They seek *allies*, recognizing that strength lies not in numbers but in our commitment to right relationships.

Survivors make good peacemakers

Howard Thurman planted a multiracial congregation in the pre-Civil Rights era. He was asked by a Hindu man on a trip to India, Why would a Black man want to be a Christian? In essence, Thurman's book *Jesus and the Disinherited* is his response to that question. He begins with the choice that Jesus faced as an impoverished member of the Jewish minority dominated by the Romans--which is the choice of the marginalized everywhere: resist or not resist?

Jesus calls the oppressors to repent. But not only that: he even calls the *marginalized* to repentance for what oppression does to them, if it leads them to resentment or hate. Why is it that the marginalized are more responsive to Jesus' call to repent than the powerful? Could it be that they have developed the skills of reconciliation *by way of their minority status*?

This is in fact how Jesus himself came by his skills as a peacemaker. The irony of Christianity is that it was a movement born in weakness that has become, in some contexts, the established religion of the powerful. Such a religion does not consider those with their backs against the wall--which is most people around the world.

In Jesus' day, nonresistance had its options. One was to capitulate and lose one's identity, like Herod and the Sadducees. Or to reduce contact with the enemy and isolate culturally, like the Pharisees.

Resistance had several options too--to take up arms (like the Zealots), or...what?

The other way of resistance was what Jesus gleaned from his Jewish heritage. This way insists that the only way to freedom is if one's emotions are not controlled by the enemy, if hate is transformed from the inside out. In this way the disinherited are freed from the dominion of the three "hounds of hell": fear, hypocrisy, and hatred. Christianity in the mind of Jesus is a technique of survival for the oppressed.[5]

A survival technique--what a transformative way of reading the Sermon on the Mount! No question of dismissing enemy love as either idealistic and unattainable on the one hand, or as capitulation and passivity to injustice on the other. Those in survival mode are ready to engage any tactic that will preserve their identity before God. And Jesus says there is really only one way to survive: transforming initiatives of peacemaking that guard the dignity of all.

Another way to frame the choice before Jesus, and before all marginalized people, is to let the pain of exclusion harden us and make us competitive, or to be softened to each others' shared grief.[6] Wherever religious minorities become peacemakers, it is because their pain has softened them to others.

Is there any other path to peacemaking but through pain? Peace cells pose some uncomfortable questions for those in the majority. Is a faith that is assumed by the surrounding culture a real faith? Or does discipleship--at least the kind that resembles a marginalized, executed Jewish peasant--require taking concrete steps toward vulnerability, freely chosen in imitation of God?

Peace cells in action

Peacemaking through pain; this is how religious minorities transform their suffering. These examples of peace cells are religious communities--Muslims in New York, Mennonite churches in Burkina Faso and Indonesia. But their salty flavor comes not only from their lively faith, but from the fact that they are bent on survival. Their stories prompt the question for all of us: what drives us toward reconciliation?

Making space: A Muslim peace cell in Harlem

After 9/11, things got difficult for Muslims living in New York City. American discourse associated Muslims with fears of violent jihad, sharia, and acts of terror. What were American Muslims to do?

One community did not have to think hard: they leaned into their identity as Muslim pacifists. They presented a different face, an alternative picture of who Muslims are. The Senegalese Sufi order known as the Murids, now spread around the world, has a long commitment to nonviolence rooted in its remarkable founder: Shaykh Amadu Bamba.

How does a Muslim pacifist group develop? Bamba and his followers reacted against both the violent jihad and the French colonial oppression they experienced. They were also shaped by a broader pacifist tradition in West Africa. [7] Before Martin Luther King, Jr., before Gandhi, Shaykh Bamba articulated a nonviolence that suffered and forgave. And his followers speak of his life and teachings in ways that Christians reserve for Jesus; in the face of an awesome military foe, he taught forgiveness as the only path to transformation.

As Murids ended up in Harlem, it is not surprising that they carried forgiveness in their DNA. When a spate of killings targeting Murid taxi drivers shocked the community in the 1990s, the Murids presented a unified front: no retaliation, only forgiveness and peacemaking. They were vulnerable--as immigrants, as religious minorities, as people doing the dangerous work no one else wanted to do. But they clung to their communal values for survival.

They survived by creating spaces that were focused on maintaining their Murid identity, even in a surrounding culture that was indifferent or even hostile. They completely abandoned the goal--so important in some Islamic political theology--of *Islamicizing* the place where they lived. Instead, they focused on thriving as minorities, like Jeremiah's call to seek the good of the city where you find yourself as strangers.

The difference between *space* and *place* is a crucial one for religious minorities. Space refers to life-giving environments of refuge and identity formation. Place is the harsh realities propped up by those who hold power, the systems that one must navigate.

Peacemakers seek space, not place. And the Murids brought a peacemaking mentality from their home in Senegal to their new home in Harlem.

The fact that nonviolent commitment is successfully passed from generation to generation is a testament to the Murids' intentionality as a peace cell. They teach their children the Murid way, and hold up Shaykh Bamba as an example whose life is relevant in any context. Religious minorities have a distinct advantage in passing along crucial moral values to children. By contrast, majorities struggle to instill a peacemaking identity in younger generations.

Murids have had to make the leap from speaking of peace in their original language of Wolof to using English. Defining concepts like peace and nonviolence across languages and cultures is not as easy as it might seem. But in the act of defining peace, we take on the position of outsiders, of peace cells, of people looking for handles that make sense to our neighbors. This practice is as fruitful for Christians as it is for Sufi Muslims.

Creating Murid spaces in Harlem resulted in something remarkable. The whole community was transformed, bit by bit--storefronts and houses were renovated, dangerous neighborhoods blossomed into spaces of fellowship, and the Murids succeeded in carving out an identity as a peace cell.[8] Their peace parades and community days are public celebrations of this transformation.

Forgiveness is miraculous, in itself and in what it produces. And forgiveness is one of the gifts that peace cells offer to the world.

A hearse for peace in Burkina Faso

What does a peace cell do in response to military coups and violent militias?

For Siaka Traoré, a Mennonite pastor in Burkina Faso, this is the pressing question. Islam has grown tremendously in West Africa. Muslims imitate Christian methods for expansion, such as youth camps, NGOs, radio stations, and social services--and it seems to be working. In Burkina Faso, where animists had been the majority, Muslims now are half the population. The country has been destabilized by coups, and active militias allied with Islamic State or al-Qaeda terrorize both Christians and Muslims.

The Mennonite church in Burkina is small. How should they respond to this crisis? For Pastor Siaka, the role for African Anabaptists is clear: they must be actively engaged in fostering a culture of peace. They cannot rely on political leadership to solve these problems. But where they can find hope is in the church.[9]

Pastor Siaka himself came to faith in Christ from a Muslim background. He brings a deep understanding and respect for Muslims. And he also wants them to find life in Christ as he did. He has worked at evangelism, Bible translation, and church planting. The most important work is building friendships with Muslim neighbors. On one occasion, the Mennonite church was constructing a new church building in a Muslim area. The long-term commitment to friendship led to Muslim neighbors joining in with the construction work![10]

Accepting help is one important practice of a peace cell. So is joining together during the times when emotions are most deeply felt--religious holidays, weddings, funerals, births, sicknesses. When Christians in Burkina mingle with Muslims at this level, they often find acceptance and respect as a religious minority. In the process of sharing joy and pain, they gain trust.

Pastor Siaka was taken aback when Muslims approached him for help in buying a hearse for the community to share. Normally Muslims would resist Christians having contact with their dead. But because of the trust they had built, they worked together to purchase the vehicle they called the Fellowship Hearse.[11]

The fruit of trust is remarkable. Muslims even seek them out for advice and help, including for the education of their children. The Burkinabé Mennonites have opened a primary school in which most of the children are from Muslim families. They have come to trust the Christians' spiritual and moral values. Muslims regularly ask Christians to lead interfaith initiatives. How does this trust happen? When peace cells take initiative to build relationships with the surrounding majority.

But minority identity is not easy to navigate. Some neighbors are convinced that Christians are actively resisting God's will. Christians represent the invasion of Western culture and civilization in Africa. For Pastor Siaka, this is why it is crucial for the Burkinabé church to demonstrate its authentic African identity and its biblical values. And the beginning place is honoring each person as created in God's image, with inestimable value.

It is a delicate calling to live among Muslims with an attitude of both respect and invitation. But there is no other way to give witness to a God who is near us, within our grasp, even to the point of taking on flesh. This fundamental character quality of God is where our witness must begin. And it is where peace cells have a distinct advantage, because they do not simply *speak* of divine vulnerability, they *enact* it.

I asked Pastor Siaka what is the most important thing in relating to Muslims. He told me, "Have integrity. Connect your actions to your words. Walk in blamelessness, justice, and fairness--these qualities speak volumes to Muslims."[12]

Peace cells see the realities below the surface. Pastor Siaka has many people say to him, "I've chosen the path of Islam--but otherwise I would like to be like you." Others confess that they would like to become Christians, but they are afraid of being seen as traitors to their faith. There is more going on in a society than is easily visible. Majorities look at surface identities--God looks at the heart (and peace cells have been given a measure of heart vision as well).

Peace cells like the church in Burkina Faso cannot afford to see Muslims as enemies, or even as competitors. Both for the sake of witness and of survival they must see their role as peacemakers and trust-builders. They avoid stereotypes, polemic, and negative images of the other.

What advice do you have for Christians in the West in relation to Muslim people? I asked Pastor Siaka.

"Approach them, and let them see Christ in you."

Powerful words from a peace cell pastor.

Good infidels: Indonesian Mennonites and Hizbullah
Peace cells knock on doors.
And keep knocking until the door is answered.

In Indonesia, Christians make up only ten percent of the population. Conflict and even violence between Muslim and Christian communities can occur. Tensions were high in the city of Solo, and militant groups were active around the region. Mennonite pastor Paulus Hartono decided to do something about it.

He knocked on the door of the leader of an Islamist paramilitary group named Hizbullah (Party of God).

This was a risky act. One newspaper referred to it as the actions of a "deranged Christian," noting that Christians and other religious minorities sensibly tend to avoid hard-line Muslims.[13]

But Pastor Paulus was not deranged; he was motivated by a desire for peace. Initially he was not well received; the first time he knocked the commander refused to speak with him. He told him, "You are a Christian and infidel, and therefore it is legitimate for us to kill you."

Who on earth would go back after such a reception? Perhaps he was a bit deranged.

Pastor Paulus did not give up, returning and knocking again and again until finally he managed to chat with the commander, drink tea, and build some trust.

But the friendship did not truly develop until the 2004 tsunami hit Aceh. Pastor Paulus invited the Hizbullah commander to join him in relief efforts. Their teams worked side by side, even sleeping in the same tents.

Another crisis hit: earthquakes destroyed thousands of homes in Central Java. Again the Mennonites and Hizbullah collaborated in rebuilding homes, mosques, and even churches.

After years of this sort of friendship, the Hizbullah commander was overwhelmed. He confessed to Pastor Paulus, "When I reflect on what we have said and done to you and other Christians, and then I witness that you and Christians have reciprocated with love and compassion, my heart has melted. Now I have realized that you Christians are good infidels."

Good infidels. Not exactly the highest compliment, but consider the speaker: a radical militia leader who has dedicated his life to defending his faith through violence and force. He is recognizing something transformative. Peace cells actually wield a force more powerful than any military: the courage that comes with love.

Jesus said, "To the one who knocks, the door will be opened" (Matt 7:8). Peace cells are not satisfied to knock on the doors of their friends. They don't only show up on the doorsteps of moderates, the people they trust to open up to them.

They knock on the doors of extremists. And sometimes, God does a miracle and the door opens.

Choosing vulnerability

Beside our house in Zanzibar was a huge baobab tree. The whole neighborhood was named after it. My most important interactions with neighborhood friends happened in the shade of its massive trunk and branches.

That spectacular tree grew from a small seed of the kind that people use to play the board game *ubao*. The Reign of God, the reign of peace, comes about from small seeds, from a little bit of yeast in the dough, from a little bit of salt in the porridge. This is the particular gift that religious minorities offer. Their survival depends on cultivating good relationships.

Recall that the tiny p-cells in our brains help us process fine details and color. In other words, p-cells turn *light* into *beauty*. So when Jesus says to his disciples, You are the light of the world--we are not simply lamps making a dark room a bit brighter. We are prisms revealing the beauty of God, casting the world in new detail and color.

Peace cells committed to Christ Jesus are not just better at evangelism than are majorities. Peace cells are the *only* evangelists in the world. This is because coercion and invitation are polar opposites. They can never go together. Either we are sharing good news, or we are putting pressure on religious outsiders. We must choose.

The path to peacemaking runs through pain, including the pain of being in the minority. To follow Jesus the Light of the world--and in turn becoming p-cells ourselves--is to take concrete, intentional steps toward vulnerability.

Christians need to be way more uncomfortable with a majority identity than we are. I want to see a deep uneasiness set in, and drive us to seek shelter from the idols of wealth and power. Faith in Jesus is a faith on the move. If we worry too much about what we will lose in the process, we lose the basic commitment of following Jesus.

Like Howard Thurman, we need to approach our faith as survivors. The test of real faith in Jesus is to have it constantly challenged by the religious identity of your neighbors.

But our survival mode is not one of hunkering down defensively. On the contrary, it's an all-out offensive against the easy pathways to enmity that our world wants to lead us down. Jesus fought this easy path tooth and nail.

Christians are a bit like manure--if you pile us up, we stink. But if you spread us around, we can do some good. The same is true of Muslims. Groupthink is powerful--and it stinks powerfully.

We see something beautiful in peace cells. A different aroma, a different flavor.

We seek to be forgiving like the Sufi Murids. Like Dorothy Grove.

We want to be creative like Pastor Siaka.

We desire to have the courage of Pastor Paulus. And of Ahmed Haile.

So what do we do if we find ourselves in the position of belonging to the same faith as our neighbors?

If you are a religious majority, find a more interesting identity. Become the person who people associate with religious minorities. Find a peace cell of people doing something out of the ordinary. Move to a place where your faith is challenged at its core.

Become a peace cell, and let a little light in. The colors are astounding.

NOTES

[1] Isaac, *The Other Side of the Wall*, 162.

[2] Hara Estroff Marano, *A Nation of Wimps: The High Cost of Invasive Parenting* (New York: Broadway, 2008), 61.

[3] Daniel Kahneman, *Thinking, Fast and Slow* (New York: Farrar, Straus, and Giroux, 2011), 135.

[4] Volf, *Exclusion and Embrace*, 100, 117, 215.

[5] Howard Thurman, *Jesus and the Disinherited* (Richmond, Indiana: Friends United Press, 1981), 12-29.

[6] DeCort, *Blessed are the Others*, 43.

[7] Jonathan Bornman, *American Murids: A Lived Muslim Practice of Nonviolence* (New York: Peter Lang, 2024), 37.

[8] Ibid., 94-95.

[9] Traore, "Afterword," in Alemu Checole et al, *Anabaptist Songs in African Hearts.* Global Mennonite History Series (Intercourse, PA: Good, 2006), 266-68.

[10]Mennonite Mission Network, "Muslims help build church in Burkina Faso," *Anabaptist World*, December 30, 2019. Available at https://anabaptistworld.org/muslims-help-to-build-a-church-in-burkina-faso/

[11] Lynda Hollinger-Janzen, "Mennonites and Muslims in Burkina Faso celebrate a unified response to suffering," Mennonite Mission Network, January 26, 2022. Available at https://www.mennonitemission.net/news/mennonites-and-muslims-in-burkina-faso-celebrate-a-unified-response-to-suffering/

[12] Siaka Traoré, email to author, October 18, 2017.

[13] "Engaging Extremists Key To Peace," *Sumanto Al Qurtuby*, May 19, 2019. Available at https://sumantoalqurtuby.com/engaging-extremists-key-to-peace/

Part II: Receiving Guests

Mustapha is one of the most exhausting people I know. About twice a week he aggressively knocks on our door. He barely utters a greeting before asking for money or medicine. He shows me cuts on his leg or sores on his feet from walking the rough streets without shoes.

Occasionally I pay him for doing some small job. More often I give him food or some article of clothing that I haven't worn in a few weeks.

Rarely does he thank me. He just informs me when he'll be back again as he takes his leave.

After a while I reached the point of peering out the window to see if it was Mustapha at the door. Could ignore the persistent knocking? Pretend I wasn't home? Did I have the energy to determine what to give him this time--particularly when I was in the middle of preparing a class or cooking a meal?

One day when Mustapha knocked I felt my patience waning. I asked God what I should do, and was immediately convicted by the Holy Spirit: *You need to change your attitude. It is not just Mustapha knocking on your door, but Jesus himself.*

From that day on, when the aggressive knock sounds I've started to say to Christy, "It's Jesus again." Something has changed in me. Rather than resentfully or dismissively engaging Mustapha, I find myself collecting items in advance to give to him when he stopped by. God has done something for my vision, to the extent that I feel joy in the opportunity to extend kindness to Mustapha, and at the same time to be visited by Jesus himself.

As I discovered, my first calling in relating to Mustapha is not to help him see Jesus rightly, but for me to *see Jesus in him.*

This may sound like a simple proposition, but it is utterly transformative of our approach to people of other faiths. It is the foundation on which good guestwork is built.

CHAPTER 6

Red-Letter Refugees

The concept of the red-letter Bible is straightforward. It highlights the words of Jesus, with the point being: pay attention to these words-- these are important!

Jesus states in Matthew 25 that he *is* the refugee.

This is a red-letter chapter. The voices of refugees are highlighted in red, to represent that they are the *voice of Jesus speaking to us*.

There is a critical test facing Christians: the mass displacement of Muslims. Will we meet the challenge as communities shaped by Jesus? Or will we succumb to the temptation to look away?

Three excuses to look away are particularly powerful.

Speed: there is no quick fix.

Distance: these problems are occurring thousands of miles away.

Innocence: it's not our fault.

These three excuses lead us away from lament. We are prone to seek quick solutions that can be wired in from afar, that require no sacrifice on our part or any recognition that we might be a part of the problem.

The spiritual practice of lament does the opposite, drawing us toward those who are most sinned against. The calling is not first of all to make a difference, but to allow ourselves to be disturbed by the pain of the encounter.[1]

This is precisely the kind of thinking that Jesus calls us to in Matthew 25. Look for me in the refugee, he says--and you will find me.

Over the last decade, the leading countries of origin for refugees to the United States are the Democratic Republic of Congo, Burma, Iraq, Syria, and Somalia.[2] Iran and Afghanistan also make the top ten list, and the number of Sudanese refugees due to civil war in Sudan is also rising--at least before travel bans blocked them. Muslim people in need of help arrive at the doorsteps of Western Christians.

Fear-driven responses such as travel bans do direct damage to one of the most compelling mission opportunities for the church in the West. The tragic effect of travel bans is that they make interfaith encounters more difficult and less likely. The goal of Christian nationalism to create a society free of the religious other is in direct opposition to the words of Jesus. The response of Christians should be to *seek out* those of other faiths in friendship, sharing our lives.

When we hear the voice of Jesus in the other, we are transformed--as individuals, as churches, and as communities. The experience of congregations in the US receiving Somali refugees offers hope. We have an opportunity to hear and respond to Jesus himself--will we take it?

Noticing Jesus as the first task

Christian witness among Muslims is hard. No Christian I've ever met has denied this. The obstacles seem insurmountable.

Muslims have deep religious commitments that are opposed to Christian doctrines about Jesus.

Cultural misunderstandings stand in the way of communicating Jesus' identity and teachings.

And history is full of open wounds--betrayals of the gospel in the Crusades, in colonial mission endeavors, and in the godless materialism and militarism of so-called Christian societies.

How can we assist Muslim neighbors to see Jesus rightly when so many things are getting in the way? What if the problem is our starting point: that mission is about *helping others* to see Jesus rightly? In fact, we have the tasks reversed! Good guestwork is not first of all about help-ing others to see Jesus. The first calling is for us to *hear and see Jesus in the vulnerable other*.

Our faithfulness to Jesus is the extent to which we are able to glimpse Jesus in the stranger--our willingness to turn the past-tense understand-ing that Jesus *was* a refugee into present-tense recognition that Jesus *is* the refugee.

Who does Jesus represent?

That Jesus *is* the refugee is a bold claim. But it is part of what it means to recognize Jesus as the mediator between humans and God.

To be a mediator is to advocate for two parties at the same time. In other words, the Messiah's representative work goes in two directions.

In one direction, Christ represents humanity to God. Hebrews 7 de-scribes Christ as a high priest interceding on our behalf. He empathizes with our sinful state and with our suffering.

In the other direction, Christ represents God to humanity as the *im-age of the invisible God* (Col 1:15). He also empathizes with our grasping in the dark for deliverance.

Jesus calls his followers to be crucified with him. This is saying some-thing remarkable: that he is not alone in representing human suffering to God and God's suffering to humanity. Crucifixion with Christ is making Christ the center of our being rather than ourselves. We are set free to see from the other's point of view.

So the meaning of the cross is a two-sided solidarity. Christ identifies God's solidarity with the victims of violence. And he also identifies the victims with God, putting them under God's protection and giving them the rights that were withheld from them.[3]

Christ identifies especially with those who are excluded, those with-out power and wealth. Dietrich Bonhoeffer is well known for resisting the Third Reich on behalf of the Jews and other victims. But Bonhoef-fer himself experienced this transformation of vision thanks to his ear-lier sojourn among African American Christians in Harlem.[4] To see

Jesus first in Black Baptists translated directly into seeing Jesus in European Jews. And transformation leads to compassionate acts of resistance and deliverance.

Nowhere is this clearer in Jesus' teaching than in the judgment passage of Matthew 25. The Human One, seated on his throne at the end of time, identifies with the hungry in need of food, the naked needing to be clothed, the sick in need of healing, and the prisoner alone in a cell.

If we jump straight to the actions that *we should be doing*--feeding the hungry, healing the sick, visiting the prisoner--we might miss the main point. We'll fall into the trap of making ourselves the heroes of the story.

The fundamental point of this teaching is that Jesus directly identifies *himself* as a hungry, naked, poor, prisoner. The first calling of the disciple, therefore, is to *see and hear* Jesus in the vulnerable other. This transformation, of identifying others with Jesus even as we recognize our own deep need for healing, is precisely how Jesus ministers to us through the hungry, the sick, and the prisoner.

For Jesus to make this the measure for judgment is remarkable. He focuses the final judgment *not* on keeping commandments, attending church, or anything else. Our vision is conforming to God's own way of viewing the world when we see Christ in people who are excluded.

And what is a sign that this transformation is occurring? When we begin to see God where we don't *want* to see God. Then we know that we are seeing with eyes that are not our own.[5]

For Jesus this is the top priority. How we relate to the poor of our world affects our salvation because it affects our relationship with God. We simply cannot know Christ and not know the poor and marginalized. To ignore those in need is to ignore Christ himself.[6]

To ignore or to pay attention to Christ is the choice facing the church in the West.

Jesus was himself a displaced person.

A Tanzanian woman told me how her family received Rwandan refugees into their home. She recalls that the father of the refugee family, bearing the burden of trauma and violence, threw back his head and sang with all his might the words of the hymn, *If ever I loved thee, my Jesus, 'tis now.*

How could he sing such words, when his life was in upheaval and chaos? Because in that moment he understood as never before the living presence of Jesus the refugee.

In the emergence of world Christianity, the attraction Jesus holds for the poor is astonishing. The margins of society are where the church grows the fastest. Something in the faith resonates with people who encounter Jesus from all corners of the world, facing all kinds of difficult economic and social situations.

What is it about Jesus that clicks for someone like this Rwandan refugee man?

The answer is that Jesus' ministry of empathic representation, his identification with the marginalized, did not emerge in a vacuum. Jesus sounds like he does in Matthew 25 because he had firsthand experience with the kind of suffering he is describing. His theology developed not in a seminary or through an abstract philosophy of justice, but out of his real lived experience as a marginalized human being. This suffering is not lost on people who encounter him in the pages of the Gospels and in the living presence of his Spirit.

Marginalized people recognize in Jesus a fellow traveler, one who can enter the perspective of others. This is difficult for those with power and privilege, but is second nature to the weak because they always have to be attuned to how their actions are perceived by the strong.[7] Those who are most excluded develop out of necessity the ocular muscles required for inverting perspective.

The beautiful irony is that the same skills allow them to enter into the perspective of Jesus as a trusted companion.[8] In the practice of learning to identify God with victims and victims with God, those who have been excluded and who have suffered the most are the teachers.

Jesus as a marginalized person connects not only with Christians, but with Muslims as well. I was invited to participate in an interfaith dialogue in Uganda, hosted by the Chancellor of a major Islamic university.

In my turn to address the multi-faith gathering I stated that the most important point of connection we have as people of faith is what we do to welcome the stranger. Why is this so important? First, our holy books dwell intensely on how God pays special attention to displaced people, to refugees, orphans, people who have lost their homes and identities. But secondly, our major prophets are displaced and vulnerable people: Abraham and Sarah the strangers in a strange land; Moses the castaway in the face of genocide; Jesus the refugee to Egypt; and Mohamed the orphan.

I then told the story of when Mohamed sent 83 members of his community to find refuge from the Meccans in the Christian kingdom of Abyssinia, in modern-day Ethiopia. When the Meccans asked King Negus to turn the refugees over to them, he protected the Muslim immigrants.[9]

This Christian's kindness is praised in several qur'anic verses. I stated before the group, "This is an important example of mutual love between Muslims and Christians." Then I sat down.

Our Muslim host stood up after me and exclaimed, "Yes it is--and it will never be forgotten!"

It's quite astounding--some seventh-century Christians extended hospitality to vulnerable Muslim neighbors, and the incident has been memorized and recited by Muslims around the world for *fourteen centuries*.

The mustard seed kind of logic that Jesus describes in Luke 13 is powerful beyond understanding. The simple transformation of seeing the stranger as a human with dignity--of seeing Jesus in the vulnerable other--yields a deeper, more significant impact than we can imagine.

Nearly a third of the world's international migrants are Muslim.[10] The amazing reality is that we have more opportunity today than ever before to tap into the mustard-seed magic of the kingdom of Jesus.

Is it safe to welcome refugees? No.

Among these 80 million displaced Muslim people, it is not difficult to imagine how such suffering can lead to extremist responses. In some individuals, the pain will find expression in radical ideologies.

It is not safe. But when has saying yes to God's will ever been safe? Welcoming the stranger and welcoming God's Word are both acts of faith--bringing something unknown, unpredictable, and uncontrollable into our lives. [11] This is not a safe thing to do.

Deciding to follow Jesus is the worst decision I have ever made, from the perspective of security and stability. As I write these words I am without a place to call home.

But here's the point: we are deluded if we think a safe option even exists. Allowing Christians and Muslims to wallow in our mutual distrust, unchallenged by the transforming power of mingling lives, is the most dangerous option of all.

Lebanon has received over a million and a half Palestinian, Iraqi, and Syrian refugees--compared to a population of only about six million. Martin Accad issues a clear call from the Middle East: "Muslims today, particularly in contexts where they are minorities, *need to have positive experiences with their Christian neighbors.* In these days of massive migration and global refugee crises, this will help them integrate better in their communities and avoid living in ghettos and environments that breed segregation and extremism."[12]

Christians in the US should be the first to decry the role their nation has played in the destabilization of refugees' countries of origin, including Afghanistan, Yemen, Iraq, and Syria. In Somalia, failed US military interventions contributed to the formation of the extremist group al-Shabaab.

But there is a better story. There is an alternative to both isolationism and intervention--good guestwork. The story of Somalis and Mennonites switching roles as guests and hosts, and the pain and miracle of that ongoing story, is a sign of hope.

Switching roles: Somali refugees and the church

In early 1953, the first Protestant workers to begin Christian work in Somalia disembarked in the capital city of Mogadishu. At the time there was no dock, so the new arrivals were precariously lowered from the ship in a basket, like Paul escaping from Damascus (Acts 9:25). These service workers were from a tight-knit community of Mennonites in Pennsylvania, awakened by a fresh calling to carry the good news of Jesus to the ends of the earth.

When they arrived, however, the Mennonites discovered that the ends of the earth were like home in surprising ways. Traditional Somali and European Mennonite cultures both emphasize genealogies, dependence on cows or camels, and oral tradition.[13] At the same time, the cultural differences were immense, not least the fact that the Mennonite Christians found themselves in a culture with a strong Islamic identity from time immemorial.

The Mennonites were welcomed as guests in the Somali home. They set up schools and clinics that shaped generations of Somalis. The road was not smooth; Mennonite Mission was dismissed from the country on several occasions, only to be welcomed back when the Cold War politics shifted. This precarious presence continued through national independence, war, dictatorship, famine, martyrdom, and nationalization of the Mennonite schools. But over time a resilient friendship was built.

Within forty years of the Mennonite arrival in Somalia, however, the roles of guests and hosts were suddenly reversed. Civil war deposed the dictator Mohamed Siad Barre, and competing warlords threw the country into chaos. This crisis, combined with devastating famine and foreign military intervention, displaced many thousands of Somalis in the early 1990s.

When Somali families began to arrive in Pennsylvania and were received there by Mennonite individuals and congregations, it was therefore the continuation of a longer story.[14]

In the decades that followed, Somalis continued to come by the thousands to the US. They were overwhelmingly young (a majority under 21 years old), most without much formal education.[15] Pull factors include not only the promise of political freedom and stability, but also the economic opportunities.

The expectations of immigrants are often checked by the harsh realities upon arrival. At the same time, many Somali refugees do find a better life in the US, running successful businesses, getting a good education, and remitting money to family members in the Horn of Africa. The 2018 congressional election brought the first Somalia-born US Representative to office, Ilhan Omar.

But new arrivals are met with overwhelming challenges. Refugees generally cycle through four stages as they learn to acclimate to their new homes. They begin with anticipation and excitement (stage 1), dreaming of a good life without worry and pain. Then the reality of adjustment sets in (stage 2), followed by culture shock and the trauma of resettlement that can produce depression and anxiety (stage 3). Many refugees finally find ways to cope and accept their new life (stage 4), but can be thrown back into other stages at different points in their journey.[16]

It is difficult for Westerners to inhabit the reality of relocating as a displaced person from the Horn of Africa to a North American context. But recognition of these stages of adjustment can provide a small glimpse into the challenges, and welcoming teams from receiving congregations observe refugee families dealing with each of these stages.

For example, reality sets in the moment a person picks up the phone. One welcoming team member commented, "We defeat non-English speakers quite quickly when public institutions are involved. When you place a call you never get a person, but a message directing you what to do."[17] The result is neglected medical appointments, prescriptions, and school activities.

Both Somali families in the stories that follow are Bantu in ethnicity, meaning that they are descendants of ethnic tribes from the Southeast coast of Africa who were captured in the nineteenth-century Arab slave trade and sold in Somalia. Bantu Somalis are ethnically and culturally distinct from the majority Somali clans and are marginalized in significant ways as a result of their slave status, including denial of access to education and other basic needs.[18]

Most Somali refugees land in economically disadvantaged neighborhoods in urban centers. It is in this context that the harsh reality and the culture shock set in. Without proficiency in English, refugees fall prey to unscrupulous landlords, cultural misunderstandings in schools and communities, and missed medical and social service appointments.

In the words Jesus (speaking through a Somali man named Abdi), **"I became frightened for Somali refugees because if I, though one of the luckiest few with a college degree and a good command of the English language, was fighting with my own demons of doubt, how would a single mother of six or more with neither the educational background nor employable skills, survive?"[19]**

For many Somali refugees, the answer to Abdi's question, "How will they survive?" has been the help of churches. Refugee resettlement agencies work hard to meet the needs of newly arrived Somalis and others. Somali families came to Pennsylvania because of the work of Church World Service (CWS), a cooperative ministry engaged in refugee resettlement.[20]

Churches play a vital role in taking on refugee families in need of help. CWS notes a huge difference in the rate of successful acclimation between families that have church sponsorship and those that do not. Without a church sponsor, families often miss appointments, find it harder to get employment, and are more likely to move away from the area.

"We cannot believe that Christians did this for us"

In 1967 a Mennonite doctor working in Somalia delivered a baby boy named Suleiman. Born into a Christian Bantu family connected to Mennonite service workers, Suleiman walked the risky path of living as a person of a minority faith in his home context. He worked with Mennonite organizations to resettle Somali Bantu families in Tanzania during the civil war in the 1990s. Receiving death threats because of his faith, by 2010 Suleiman could not continue to live in East Africa.

The doctor who delivered Suleiman, now retired and living in Pennsylvania, and having had no connection to Suleiman since his birth, caught word from a mission agency that Suleiman and his family were in danger and needed to relocate. The doctor's congregation, Springfield Mennonite Church, sprang into action to form a welcoming team. According to a CWS worker, the team essentially took over the task of resettling the family.[21]

Springfield has a history of sponsoring refugee resettlement, and the welcoming team was well prepared when the Juba family of four arrived. The team found a house, furnished it with help from the congregation, drove them to appointments, and made school arrangements for the children.

The church included resettlement expenses in the budget and paid the family's rent for a year. Whenever household items were needed, church members quickly responded, and one person even donated a small car. As one welcoming team member put it, "With Suleiman's family, we were on 24-7 call if there was a problem."[22]

One major factor in the successful acclimation of the Juba family was the fact that as Christians they were able to plug directly into congregational life from the outset. Although Suleiman's wife had no English upon arrival, the family began attending Sunday services, participating in a Sunday School class and other church events.

The Juba family has been an important part of congregational revitalization. Suleiman agrees; "Many people did not know about Somalis or had negative views, but now they have learned from us who Somalis are. And they are now awaiting any Somali family. They keep asking me if I know anyone who is coming."[23]

From refugee to mission worker

Finding work is a major challenge for refugees, and for Suleiman the difficulty was compounded by the fact that he has lost one of his legs. His ability in Somali, Swahili, English, and Bantu Somali languages provided him with some part-time translation work.

But from the moment he arrived in the United States there was other work to be done; Suleiman knew personally the experience of being a refugee, and he felt the Holy Spirit guiding him to be helpful to other struggling Somali families.

Springfield donated a van, and before long Suleiman had a driver's license and was transporting Somali refugees to medical and school appointments, Somali stores, and wherever they needed to go.

Suddenly Suleiman, as a refugee sponsored by Springfield Mennonite Church, was the liaison between the Somali refugee community and their new host culture!

Suleiman's role in the community goes far beyond logistics; he observes Somali refugees in all stages of adjustment. The dreams of an easy life in the US are quickly shattered, and confusion, depression, and anxiety become powerful traps without someone like Suleiman to answer questions and provide encouragement.

As an ambassador between the communities, Suleiman is often privy to the ways that deeply held assumptions are challenged. He has been told by Muslim families, **"What we believed before was that Christians are our enemies. But when we came to the US that idea was washed out--now we know that they are not enemies but are helpful to us."**

For some Somali Muslims, interacting with Christians is a stretch, let alone setting foot in a church building. Yet in spite of this barrier, Suleiman has Muslim friends who join him on occasion in attending Springfield's worship services.

Suleiman's ministry also extends around the world. He has regular contact with Somali believers in different corners of the globe, some of whom he has never met in person. His contact with believers around the world by phone and internet constitutes a worldwide fellowship.

In turn, Suleiman keeps Springfield abreast of what is happening in Somalia. Suleiman has received a powerful calling and ministry to Somali immigrants. He attributes this calling directly to Jesus, stating, **"Let churches follow the way Jesus said himself: to receive those who are new, to not discriminate. I learned from Springfield how to do that."**[24]

This is Jesus' yeast metaphor in Matthew 13:33 in action: a congregation's simple but intentional ministry to one family has impacted both the local community and individuals around the world.

But the impact was to become even greater. A Christian family is one thing. But what if the refugee family is Muslim?

"We cannot believe that Christians did this for us"
When the escalating Syrian crisis hit the news, it sparked an interest in another church in the area, Oak Creek.[25]

Although several members of the congregation had served in Somalia, Oak Creek expected to sponsor a Syrian family. But when CWS connected them with a Somali Bantu family, the response was, "This is who God brought us!" [26]

The church formed a welcoming committee consisting of ten members with experience in different areas: medical, financial, and educational. One member observes, "For those of us not called to go overseas, this is a way to be the hands and feet of Jesus here at home." [27]

Suleiman was delighted to discover that he knew the family from a neighboring village in Somalia. He met them at the airport, and everyone was overwhelmed with joy. From the moment of their arrival, the Gosha family was blessed with both a supporting church and a cultural interpreter in Suleiman.

Like Springfield, Oak Creek pulled together as a congregation to set up a house for the Gosha family before they arrived. On the very Sunday that the welcoming team posted a signup sheet with all kinds of household needs, everything was provided.

The family continues to practice their Islamic faith, but several months after their arrival they attended one Sunday service at Oak Creek in order to introduce themselves and to express their gratitude from the pulpit. *Only at that point* did the Gosha family fully realize that the people helping them had been a *church* – not just a well-meaning group of people! The family later participated in the church's community day event.

For two weeks after the Gosha family's arrival, the welcoming team was at their home every day. While CWS made all the initial connections for medical appointments and all the government requirements, the team did virtually everything else for them.

After the initial move, the team's involvement with the family settled into three categories.

First, a team member stops in regularly to spend time with the three pre-teen daughters--playing games, cooking, visiting local sites, helping with school work or English skills.[28]

Second, the team helps with medical and school-related appointments.

Third, one member works with the father of the family on banking, budgeting, and paying bills. The goal is to foster more self-sufficiency; as the family becomes more independent, the number of team members required to keep up with appointments decreases.[29]

Resettlement to the US has been difficult for the Gosha family. At one point one of the daughters disappeared, only to emerge in another part of the country with a man. When this happened, according to Suleiman, the family surely would have left the area were it not for the church's full-on support. They told him, "We cannot believe that Christians did this for us."

These moments of recognition are the power of the gospel--to experience Jesus at work in the world is to touch the miraculous.

Only concrete acts of love and hospitality--good guestwork---can break through the impossible barriers of hostility.

Trivial is radical: Refugees and mission

Some churches find it easy to imagine mission with Somalis along traditional lines of sending workers to a majority-Somali context. Congregations and prove willing to invest huge amounts of training, personnel, and financial resources within the sending paradigm.

Would these churches welcome the Muslims who are coming to their doorsteps, often with deep needs for assistance and friendship?

Hospitality toward refugees comes with practice. Cities that have successfully resettled one refugee group are better equipped to assist other groups.[30] The same is true for churches; once a congregation has become attuned to the specific needs of new arrivals, the DNA of the community changes irreversibly. A church that receives refugees will not experience it as a one-time endeavor, but rather becomes a kind of community that practices such hospitality.

When our family moved to Somaliland, people in our sending congregations sometimes asked us what they could do to help. Our response was always this: Simply make friends with the Somalis who are in your hometown, either as newly arrived refugees or as a more established community. The Somali grapevine is so effective that our neighbors in Hargeisa are likely acquainted with your Somali neighbors in the US.

The way we treat refugees matters: for mission at home and abroad, for the sake of obedience to Jesus the refugee, and for the goal of a better world.

The challenge of faithful witness is one that every congregation does and should wrestle with. The fact that relating to a refugee family complicates those questions is actually a blessing, because simple acts of friendship take on much greater significance. The small moments of sharing life can turn out to be the most profound ministry of all. After years of relating to Somali Bantu refugees, one worker observes, "The ministries I once thought so trivial I now think are the most radical."[31]

What emerges is conversion--of hearts, of vision, of congregational life--as a genuine sense of mutuality develops. In both these cases, the language and worldview of the congregations' welcoming teams shifted over time from a paternalistic framework to one of mutuality. In theological terms, the shift could be described as away from "being the hands and feet of Jesus" toward an understanding of the refugee as an agent of change. A team member at Springfield comments, "We are *not* to demonstrate a patronizing spirit toward the refugees coming to us needing help...but to develop a relationship which is a *mutual blessing* in which we value and respect their lives and culture and what they can teach us."[32]

Transformed vision--the invitation of Jesus to recognize his very self in the refugee--is a gift beyond measure, waiting for churches to reach out and receive it.

The red-letter refugees in this chapter are the very voice of Jesus speaking to the churches.

Jesus confesses in Matthew 25, with Abdi: **"I was frightened, plagued by doubt, and displaced."**

Jesus reaches out in hope to those who claim his name, with Suleiman: **"The Christians—who did not know me before—now know who I am."**

Jesus speaks in the voice of the Gosha family: **"I cannot believe that Christians, who were my enemies, did this for me."**

Jesus is actively injecting himself into the story of our lives, through the presence of refugees. But he doesn't stop there. He invites us to *read ourselves*--and our Muslim neighbors--into the very pages of Scripture.

To engage in a little bit of name-calling.

NOTES

[1] Emmanuel Katongole and Chris Rice, *Reconciling All Things: A Christian Vision for Justice, Peace and Healing* (Downers Grove, IL: InterVarsity, 2008), Kindle edition, location 900.

[2] Noah Schofield and Amanda Yap, *Refugees: 2023 Immigration* (U.S. Department of Homeland Security, November 2024), 6. Available at https://ohss.dhs.gov/sites/default/files/2024-11/2024_1108_ohss_refugee_annual_flow_report_2023.pdf

[3] Volf, *Exclusion and Embrace*, 70, 272, 22-23.

[4] Reggie Williams, *Bonhoeffer's Black Jesus: Harlem Renaissance Theology and an Ethic of Resistance* (Waco: Baylor University Press, 2014).

[5] Richard Rohr, *Everything Belongs: The Gift of Contemplative Prayer* (New York: Crossroad Publishing Company, 2003), 58.

[6] Engdahl, *Great Chasm*, location 215.

[7] Miroslav Volf, "Living with the 'Other,'" in J. Dudley Woodberry, Osman Zümrüt, and Mustafa Köylü, eds., *Muslim and Christian Reflections on Peace: Divine and Human Dimensions* (Lanham, MD: University Press of America, 2005), 13-15.

[8] Glen Harold Stassen, *A Thicker Jesus: Incarnational Discipleship in a Secular Age* (Louisville: Westminster John Knox, 2012), 172-73.

[9] Karen Armstrong, *Muhammad: A Biography of the Prophet* (London: Phoenix, 1991), 122.

[10] Stephanie Kramer and Yunping Tong, "The Religious Composition of the World's Migrants," (Pew Research Forum Report, August 19, 2024), available at https://www.pewresearch.org/religion/2024/08/19/muslim-migrants-around-the-world/.

[11] Tobias Brandner, "Hosts and Guests: Hospitality as an Emerging Paradigm in Mission," *International Review of Mission* 102, no. 1 (2013): 96-98.

[12] Accad, *Sacred Misinterpretation*, 342. Emphasis mine.

[13] Bertha Beachy, "My Pilgrimage in Mission," *International Bulletin of Missionary Research* 35 (2011), 208-212.

[14] For the purpose of confidentiality, the names of the congregations and individuals involved in these case studies, both Somali and North American, have been changed or initialized.

[15] State Department Bureau of Population, Refugees and Migration's Refugee Processing Center, available at https://cis.org/Rush/Somali-Refugees-US.

[16] D.L. Mayfield, *Assimilate or Go Home: Notes from a Failed Missionary on Rediscovering Faith,* Kindle edition (New York: HarperCollins, 2016), Kindle edition, location 79.

[17] R.H. (Oak Creek Welcoming Team), email message to author, November 15, 2016.

[18] Sandra M. Chait, *Seeking Salaam: Ethiopians, Eritreans, and Somalis in the Pacific Northwest,* (Seattle: University of Washington Press, 2011), Kindle edition, location 22. Mayfield explains, "The Somali Bantu are a people who have been kicked in the teeth by the world....When the violence broke out between the warring tribes and clans in Somalia, the Bantu were the first to feel shocks--much of their farming and agriculture was taken, or burned, unspeakable acts were done to the women and children, and so many men were killed." (Mayfield, *Assimilate or Go Home*, location 442).

[19] Ahmed I. Yusuf, *Somalis in Minnesota,* (St. Paul, MN: Minnesota Historical Society, 2012), Kindle edition, locations 365-68.

[20] The approach of CWS is to connect refugee families with congregations that can facilitate their adjustment to the new context. CWS faces an overwhelming number of refugees, and thus can only provide support to new families for three months. Furthermore, the services CWS provides are distributed among all the clients, limiting the attention to any given family unit. Families receive an orientation of three to five days upon arrival, which is not nearly enough time to navigate a new social system, and in some cases language translation is unavailable

[21] B.W., Skype interview by author, September 30, 2016.

[22] I.L. and M.E.L. (Springfield Welcoming Team), Skype interview by author, October 9, 2016.

[23] Suleiman Juba, Skype interview by author, September 25, 2016.

[24] Juba, interview.

[25] S.S. (Pastor, Oak Creek Mennonite Church), email message to author, November 15, 2016.

[26] Oak Creek Mennonite Church Welcoming Team, Skype interview by author, November 13, 2016.

[27] K.H. (Oak Creek Welcoming Team), email message to author, November 16, 2016.

[28] A.G. (Oak Creek Welcoming Team), email message to author, November 14, 2016.

[29] L.N. (Oak Creek Welcoming Team), email message to author, November 14, 2016.

[30] For example, Minneapolis resettled Southeast Asian refugees in the 1970s, which enabled the city to set up the social services later used by Somali refugees. Yusuf, *Somalis in Minnesota*, location 694.

[31] Mayfield, *Assimilate or Go Home*, location 2515.

[32] M.E.L. (Springfield Welcoming Team), email message to author, October 9, 2016.

CHAPTER 7

Seeing Samaritans

Whenever my children play imaginative games, the main question becomes: *Who are you going to be?* My son Felix has an array of masks and costumes for any scenario, to remind everyone involved of *who is who.*

As adults, we learn to ask this question much more quietly. After all, social hierarchy, power imbalances, cross-cultural relationships--these are tricky and potentially awkward dynamics to navigate.

Perhaps the solution is to eliminate labels. Labels are signs of prejudice, serving only to create and sustain divisions.

But we cannot stop our brains from working this way – either as children or as adults. We think symbolically, about ourselves and others. What if the reality is that *we don't label each other enough--we just need better labels?*

We learn by analogy. Jesus recognizes this, which is why he loved stories. So did the Gospel writers--that's why they spend so little ink on theology, and so much about what Jesus did and said. Stories are so important because we're all asking when we come to the Bible: Who am I in this story?

It's the right question to be asking.

That's precisely why the passages about Samaritans are so interesting. Who are they to Jesus?

The Samaritans were for Jesus and his disciples what *Muslims are for Christians today*. Muslims are our Samaritans.

They are the other--our religious rivals. We are very close in some ways. We are far apart in others. And *very* far apart, often, in our loyalties--in our sense of competition and even in our mutual hostility.

It's all there in the Bible, in the Samaritan passages.

The religious competition of Jesus' day is one that he chose not to ignore but to take on explicitly--and to turn on its head. Jesus' audience, including his disciples, must have found the parable of the Good Samaritan repulsive, since the Samaritan represents profanity, even non-humanity, enmity not only of Jews but also of God. The Samaritan has a negative religious value.[1]

For many Christians and Muslims today, the other has a negative religious value. Especially in majority-Christian contexts, where Muslims are marginalized guests, Christians need to rediscover the power of name-calling. Not of the harmful, derogatory sort--but the transformative, surprising kind of labeling that Jesus engaged in.

Kenyan Christians are already doing it.

Shifta or Samaritan?

In December 2015 members of the militant group al-Shabaab stopped a bus in northern Kenya. The attackers ordered the passengers off the bus and demanded that the Muslims and Christians separate.

One year earlier, in November 2014, there had been a similar incident in which al-Shabaab stopped a bus with sixty passengers, half Muslims and half Christians, on their way to Nairobi from northern Kenya. They separated the Christians from the Muslims and shot the Christians to death.

So when attackers again stopped a bus near the Somali border a year later and made the same demands, everyone knew what was about to happen. The Muslim women quickly shared their Islamic garments (*hijab* and *buibui*) with the Christian women, so that the attackers could not determine the religious identity of the women.

The militants then asked the men to disembark, but the Muslim men in turn also refused to separate along religious lines. According to one of the Muslim passengers who was injured in the attack, Sabdow Salah Farah, "We started quarrelling with them and told them they were not doing the right thing. We then asked them to kill everyone in the bus or leave us alone."[2]

It was risky for all of them, as al-Shabaab's reputation for brutal killing was well established. But the Muslims protected their Christian neighbors, and one Muslim man even lost his life in the attack.

The really notable part of this story is that--without consultation ahead of time--all the Muslims had to agree to this rescue plan. Every single one had to put their life on the line. If some had backed out or disagreed, the plan would have failed.[3]

There is a new standard for *neighborliness*, set in this case by Muslims, reflecting the best in both faith traditions--to love and obey God, and to love and protect one's neighbor.

This incident poses a real-life parable of the sort that Jesus might tell to Christians today. The parable culminates in the question, "Who were neighbors to those who fell into the hands of the robbers?" (Luke 10:36). The answer, of course, is the character Jesus puts forward as worth imitating: the religious other.

What are Kenyan Christians supposed to do with this incident? Faced with the challenge of a religious minority whose roots are in a neighboring country, how do they understand Somalis symbolically?

There are at least two options (which both make an appearance in Jesus' parable): *shifta* (bandit) or Samaritan. *Shifta* is the East African word for bandits who take advantage of the more difficult to govern areas of the region (such as the northern Kenyan province close to Somalia). This is much like the rough, ungoverned terrain that Jesus describes.

The second option is to see Somalis as *Samaritans*. But these are both labels, both a kind of name-calling. What might it look like to engage in *positive* name-calling?

The history of Kenya shows just how significant a shift this is. When ethnic Somalis in northern Kenya attempted to secede and join the pan-Somali movement in the 1960s, the Kenyan government labeled the conflict the "Shifta War" as part of a propaganda effort. Leaders know the power of stirring up hate and distrust against an enemy.

By the time a ceasefire was brokered in 1967, the violence between Kenyan forces and Somali militia groups had killed thousands of people. Kenyan counter-insurgency forces had created concentration camps for Somalis, killed livestock, and permanently disrupted Somali traditional ways of life.

It was in this context of trauma and war that Kenyans, following the agitprop of their government, began to use the epithet *shifta* not only for secessionists but for *all Somalis*.

Some Kenyan Christians were taken in by the officially sanctioned hatred.

But the gospel has power to break through even the most virulent propaganda.

A new metaphor for enemies, from open hostility to evangelization, is a positive development. There are many reasons for this shift, including demographic changes, economic partnership, and religious motivations of evangelization and peacebuilding.

What do Kenyan Christians mean when they apply the Samaritan label to Somalis?

One meaning is in response to Acts 1:6-11, in which Jesus promises the disciples that they will receive power to be witnesses in Jerusalem, Judea, Samaria, and the ends of the earth. A Kenyan evangelical Lutheran leader stated, "Our Samaritans are the Somalis. Oh yes, we must receive power from the Spirit to reach them." This conversation took place as he and others were preparing to preach the gospel to Muslims through vision clinics co-sponsored by the Kenyan government and the Evangelical Lutheran Church of Kenya.

So part of the move from *shifta* to Samaritan is that Kenyan evangelicals begin to see Somalis still as *other*, but as capable of conversion to Christ.[4]

Another meaning for the Samaritan metaphor is the emphasis on kinship and reconciliation. In the words of one Christian truck driver who was near a major mall when terrorist attacks occurred, "Somali and Kenyan Muslims are still our cousins. Borders can divide us, but we are still extended family."[5]

The language of family applied across religious lines is powerful. It can cause mythically based conflict, such as the competition for the status of favored son between Isaac and Ishmael. Or it can shape the imagination in a peacemaking direction.[6] This truck driver seems to be moving toward peace when he speaks of Muslims as family.

A third possible meaning for the label is to see Somalis as potential Samaritans like the one in Jesus' parable in Luke 10. One Kenyan Christian gave the example of a Nairobi cab driver named Sa'id, whom he had observed helping a woman who had been in a car accident. This led him to reflect that Somalis "may prove to be a surprising source of God's blessing."[7]

Clearly these Kenyans are reading their Bibles. These three interpretations correspond to three prominent New Testament depictions of Samaritans.

The first sees Samaritans as a middle ring in the outward expansion of the gospel, part of the whole world to which Jesus commissions his followers to witness (Acts 1).

The second records Jesus' conversation with the Samaritan woman, over the kinship of Jews and Samaritans--and the Messiah who transcends both religious systems (John 4).

The third, in Luke 10, is the most powerful example of the three of *subversive othering*. What do I mean by that? It still recognizes Samaritans as the religious *other*. But if the parable fulfils its purpose, it undermines our theological, social, and physical territoriality. It has a transformative effect.

Labeling has the power to build peace.

The risks of name-calling

Should we follow this example of name-calling more broadly?

We've seen that red-letter refugees represent the voice of Jesus speaking to us.

But in the context of displacement, might we see our Muslim neighbors through the New Testament lens of the category of Samaritan? This leads us to several important questions.

First, *is it helpful to think symbolically about the religious other?* Christians have been reading Muslims into the Bible for a long time: as the Pharisees, as militant groups like the Assyrians and the Babylonians; as hypocrites, magicians, or the poor and oppressed.

What a complicated endeavor--not least because every group has a spectrum of human personalities! So is it even worth trying to lump people together?

Christians often see Muslims in three places: Cornelius, the woman at the well, and the disciples on road to Emmaus. Furthermore, Christians often see Islam collectively in the Bible as the religion of Abraham, the religion of the prophets from Adam to Jesus, or even as the Antichrist of 1 John or the Beast of Revelation.[8]

Why is this impulse to see each other symbolically such a strong one? Most religions express a felt need to exclude at some level, to create some kind of other, and to maintain boundaries.

But is this a *religious* phenomenon? Religion is an easy target for criticism. But drawing boundaries is universal human behavior. Societies exist because of the othering that holds them together. The church and state are separate because only certain forms of othering are wrong. It would be a mistake to lump all forms of othering together, when the Abrahamic faiths are all built on the concept of a *community of believers*.[9]

In other words, religious othering is a fundamental feature of faith and practice, shaped by powerful metaphors and images. We all think symbolically about the world. What we need is not to discard such metaphors altogether, but to find ones that are transformative toward peace and mutuality.

But from a young age we are taught that calling names is not nice. Should we not rather be focusing on what we share in common?

So the next question we need to ask is: *How might applying the label of Samaritan in Muslim-Christian relations be unhelpful?* [10]

There are two ways in which the language can undermine the quest for peace with displaced Somalis and Kenyan Muslims. One interpretation of the Samaritan is that of an object for preaching, a lost and sinful person who is still capable of responding to Christ. The Somali then becomes not simply the enemy, but a neighbor with whom one interacts for the purpose of conversion and redemption.

Clearly preaching is better than demonizing. But the ongoing competition--for numbers, for educational and political influence--only exacerbates the centuries-long conflict between Somalis and Kenyans, and between Muslims and Christians.[11] As believers, we need something better than competition if we seek to build peace.

Another criticism of this metaphor is that it is territorial. The idea of a Christian nation can only emerge out of a Christendom mentality, in which religion takes on a territorial dimension.[12] Christendom habits die hard. When the Samaritan metaphor is superimposed onto this worldview--as if first you conquer Jerusalem, then Judea, then finally you get to Samaria--it only reinforces territorial assumptions.

In Kenya, the Christendom mentality can look like assuming that to be Kenyan is to be Christian, and conflating Somali with Muslim (despite the fact that around eleven percent of Kenyans are Muslims, not only those of Somali background). In that sense, the Samaritan metaphor serves to prop up the narrative that Kenya is a Christian country.

For example, Kenyan evangelicals involved in an eye clinic in a Muslim neighborhood were presenting the gospel to Muslims. They were trying to demonstrate that good health goes along with Christian faith. But the program was run through President Uhuru Kenyatta's *Kenya Vision 2030* plan. In other words, they were attempting to convert Muslims at the clinic not only to the way of Christ, but also to the way of Kenya.[13]

When viewed as *shifta*, Somalis/Muslims are incapable of integration into Kenyan space. As Samaritans, what changes is that integration is a possibility (with qualifications): *if* they convert to Christianity, adapt to Christian norms, and lose the qualities that make them other.[14] The Somali as Samaritan can choose to integrate or not.

Mixing religious metaphors with politics is not transformative. Any othering that is territorial, or exists to exert control over the political, social, or economic spheres is not the sort of subversive metaphor that Jesus has in mind.

Labeling is dangerous. It can prop up systems that are meant to exclude.

And yet it is universal behavior, and Jesus himself engaged in it.

Like Jews and Samaritans, Muslims and Christians cannot avoid one another. In Kenya alone, there are over 300,000 Somali refugees.[15] If labeling one another is a dangerous practice, it is far less perilous than pretending the interfaith conflicts do not exist.

Jesus did not ignore Samaritans. He initiated contact with the Samaritan woman. He traveled through their territory with intentionality. He included a Samaritan in his healing ministry in Luke 17 (and the foreigner turned out to be the only one to say thank you). He introduced them into his parables--when he really didn't need to mention them. The Good Samaritan could have been just *some guy*, and still be a good story.

There is a Samaritan passage in the New Testament that I haven't yet mentioned. But it is perhaps the most significant one of all.

At the beginning of his journey to Jerusalem (Luke 9:51-56), Jesus experiences Samaritan opposition. The disciples are furious--they wish to pray down fire from heaven to destroy the town.

What terrible disciples! I would never ask the Lord to do something like that. Would I?

Three heads on fire

Three times the Bible mentions fire coming down upon heads. I would love to say that I've only ever wished for two out of three.

If there is ever a prize established for the *Worst Field Trip*, I might have a winner.

I was teaching a course on Islam and Christianity at a seminary in Ethiopia. The dozen students in the class were mostly pastors, some working in majority-Muslim areas of Ethiopia. I asked how many had ever been inside a mosque. Only one person raised his hand.

So I decided it was important for us to visit a mosque during prayer, to be there as learners and to hear from the Muslims who were gathered there why their faith was important to them.

I found the closest mosque in the town and tracked down the imam. Unfortunately, I don't speak Amharic, and he had no English. A passerby did his best to translate for us. I told the imam that I was hoping to visit his mosque, just to observe and understand. Would that be all right? He indicated that it was.

When I told the class we were going to visit the mosque, one of my students was a bit alarmed. He said to me, "You need to understand the situation here in Ethiopia. Muslims and Christians don't interact like that." The other students were supportive of the idea, and the leadership of the seminary approved the trip as well.

I felt anxiety about the encounter. So I returned to the mosque and again spoke to the imam about our upcoming visit. Again, he seemed open to the idea, and other men who were there for prayer were very welcoming, even inviting me to pray with them.

But I still worried. I spent more time in prayer than I had in a long time. I said to God, *What am I doing? I'm an outsider, a Westerner, a young teacher butting his head into a situation where a fragile tolerance exists between the Orthodox Christians and the Muslims and the evangelicals.*

The other part of me replied, *If we can't step out in faith and try to understand each other and to be a good neighbor to the other, then what good is it to talk about peacemaking?*

Is that you, Holy Spirit? Sometimes it's hard to tell.

We piled into a van and drove to the mosque on the day of the appointment. I could tell that the students were nervous--this was really out of the ordinary for them.

As we were entering the mosque, we were met by the imam.

He was furious.

Through my students I understood that he was saying, *You're coming here to try to teach us, and to convert us to Christianity, and I'm supposed to let you just walk in here?*

I was dismayed, and so were my students. At that moment I realized what a poor job my translator had done. I apologized profusely, and did my best to clarify that we were simply coming to learn. But by then the whole thing was a wash.

I sure hope no one wrote a course review that day.

We went back to the classroom and I took a deep breath. We were all shell-shocked from the encounter. *What have I done?* I thought. If anyone in the class had been inclined to reach out in friendship to Muslim neighbors, there went that idea.

In that moment, the disciples' response to the Samaritan opposition did not feel so extreme.

Look--we came in peace, just as guests, seeking a better understanding and a deeper relationship--and *we were treated this way*? The kind of anger the imam displayed toward us makes you angry in return--and confused, and disoriented. That's surely how the disciples were feeling.

Even more, they felt it on behalf of Jesus. Who would protect and vindicate their gentle, nonviolent teacher?

The disciples' vicarious anger made them project their feelings onto Jesus. They didn't confess to him, *Being treated like this makes me want to destroy these Samaritans.* Because they didn't own that impulse, they instead forced it on Jesus--"Do you want us to call fire down on them?"

Imagine how Jesus would have responded if they had said instead, *We are feeling wounded, and it makes us want to wish them harm.* It would have made all the difference. He would not have rebuked them. He would have healed them.

Some manuscripts add, "Lord, do you want us to call fire down from heaven to destroy them, *just as Elijah did?*" Doubtless the disciples are referring to the showdown between Elijah and the prophets of Baal on Mount Carmel (1 Kings 18). That confrontation ended with Elijah slaughtering his enemies, after being vindicated by fire from heaven.

So the disciples don't just have the moral high ground of being treated offensively--they also have a powerful precedent to appeal to. They're asking Jesus, *Do you want to be a great prophet like Elijah? Go ahead, destroy your enemies. You are within your rights.*

This is where our minds go when we're wounded. Look what they did to us--and also look what these others did too--and there's really no difference between the Samaritans and the servants of Baal. We would be totally justified in treating them just as this respectable prophet did before.

That's the *first fire on heads*, the way the disciples meant it--destruction, payback, justified and with precedent.

So that's the space we were in, sitting in silence in the classroom in Ethiopia after this heated confrontation.

The oldest member of the class, a seventy-year-old seasoned pastor, broke the silence. "We started this seminar by talking about one of the major challenges – misunderstanding one another. And here we have just experienced a perfect example. We were misunderstood, and we were met with great anger as a result. But all that we are called to do is reach out in friendship the best way we know how. And that's what we did."

There was a collective sigh of relief in the room. The Holy Spirit lifted from us the burden of making things turn out right. And lifted from me the shame of having organized the *Worst Field Trip Ever*. We were gently reminded that we only need to do what the Spirit of love is leading us to do. There is no guarantee that we will be received one way or another.

I have been warmly welcomed by Muslims in enough different contexts that I hoped we would be received with openness that day. But stepping out in faith demands that kind of uncertainty.

Paul writes that uncertainty is just a part of what it means to deal with rivals. "Do not take revenge. On the contrary: 'If your enemy is hungry, feed him; if he is thirsty, give him something to drink. In doing this, you will heap burning coals on his head.' Do not be overcome by evil, but overcome evil with good" (Rom 12:19-21).

This is the *second kind of fire on heads*: pricking the conscience of the other. Appealing to our shared humanity, our shared dignity, is like bringing down fire – with hope for healing and reconciliation.

On my visit to Iran, I was struck by how much shared dignity and shared humanity is awaiting us--if we can only find ways to mingle our lives! The ideology of separation is what leads to sentiments like what the disciples expressed. I doubt that they had Samaritan friends--the people of the village where Jesus was rejected were just a nameless blob, somehow less than human.

As I write this, the Israeli military, with the help of the United States, is literally raining down fire on the heads of Iranian men, women, and children. It is not just a fantasy voiced by frustrated disciples. It is real. And it's where that sort of thinking leads.

Jesus knows this, and that's why he rebukes the disciples--don't let that attitude have any space in your head or your heart, because it will certainly lead to action.

There is a *third fire on heads* in Scripture--the arrival of the Holy Spirit at Pentecost. Here we see the true desire of Jesus, the reason that he rebuked the disciples. He has a much better vision of what fire on heads can do. Fire is meant to give power for God's mission in the world.

At Pentecost people from all different regions and languages are named. In fact, the first three names are Parthians, Medes, and Elamites, which refer to modern-day Iran! Iranians are the first God-fearing people named at Pentecost. The church in Iran was born at Pentecost, and continues to this day.

So who are we in this story? If we are honest, we're the disciples. We need to be corrected--because Jesus is lovingly leading us away from Mount Carmel and toward Pentecost, from the fire of revenge to the fire of a pricked conscience to the fire of the Spirit of God.

The unexpected benefits of name-calling

When we are in the religious majority, what we need from Scripture is *disruption*. There are lots of potential metaphors in Scripture, waiting to help us find ourselves in the story. Is there a way to determine that the labels we apply to others are transformative (and not harmful)?

The power of the Samaritan metaphor is that it sneaks up on us, surprising us with meanings that we did not intend to appropriate. This is the effect of Jesus' life and teaching – to catch off guard, to turn expectations upside-down, to make the last first.

How do we recognize a subversive metaphor, as opposed to one with ulterior motives, propping up our privilege? There are three simple tests.

First, *does the label challenge religious assumptions?*

All the stories and parables about Samaritans represent Jesus' refusal to embrace the vengeful sentiments of his compatriots. Jesus directly confronted Jewish prejudice toward Samaritans, casting the hero of parable as a despised other, while portraying two of his own faith's leaders as villains.

David Bosch takes it one step further, arguing that in many of the New Testament stories, "salvation is ultimately tied to the person of Jesus.... He is the Samaritan, who takes pity on his Jewish archenemy."[16] To his fellow Jews, he was saying, *To you I am a Samaritan*. He is not telling his Jewish hearers to convert to Samaritan religion, but rather to have their ethical thinking shaped by looking beyond their religious categories.

In our day, he is saying, *To you I am a Muslim*.

The context of the parable gives an astonishing insight. It is the culmination of Jesus' teaching on hospitality. But notice the questions that prompted it all: *What can I do to inherit eternal life? How do I fulfill the law?*

According to Jesus, *interfaith hospitality is a fulfillment of the law*. Amos Yong asks, "Might people of other faiths not only be instruments through which God's revelation comes afresh to the people of God, but also perhaps be able to fulfill the requirements for inheriting eternal life...precisely through the hospitality that they show to their neighbors (which includes Christians)?"[17]

If our response is to say, "Wait a minute – Samaritans/Muslims do not inherit eternal life just by being good neighbors to us!"--then we need to ask whether we are taking our cues from the mouth of *Jesus* or from the people who challenged him.

Jesus' portrayal of the Samaritan/Muslim as fulfilling God's law shakes our religious categories. And that's exactly his intention.

We need not worry that such a reading is not evangelical enough. If anything, it's *more* evangelical than what we usually practice. The motivation is clear: Go become the guest of Muslims to give them an opportunity to inherit eternal life!

As we become guests of Muslims, we give them a chance to welcome us, to bind our wounds, to sacrifice their time and resources on our behalf. In other words, we extend an invitation for them to fulfill God's law in the same way that the Samaritan did--and in so doing inherit eternal life.

And we pray that we would also fulfill the law by extending hospitality to needy people of other faiths--which leads us to the second test.

Second, *does the label invite repentance?*

Jesus' shocking use of a hostile category of people challenges virtue-by-belonging. One of the primary ways we violate the dignity of people of other faiths is to identify behavior by *some* and make it essential to the character of the group.

For example, when Ethiopia (with the backing of the US) invaded Somalia in 2006, the tanks rolled into Mogadishu on Christmas Day. With the goal of regime change, the Ethiopian military was not taking prisoners. Many civilians were killed.

A British journalist recounted that Somalis were looking around at the damage and the thousands of dead, and the widespread sentiment was, "This is the work of Christian Ethiopians. Muslims wouldn't do anything like this."[18]

Of course we know that some Muslims can and do kill, just as some Christians do. The error of deeming groups as essentially incapable of good or evil becomes more obvious when it is unfairly applied to us. This story rightly provokes a reaction from Christians. But it also demonstrates that we must be careful to direct scrutiny toward ourselves even as we judge the actions of others. And we must always compare the *best* of our respective faiths as a practical way to love our Muslim neighbors as we love ourselves.

Jesus' rebuke to his disciples who wanted revenge calls Christians to repent for our own anger and hatred toward Muslims. Jesus then tells his disciples to turn that anger into repentance (Luke 10:13-16) before relating the parable of the Good Samaritan. The connection is unambiguous; Samaritans are the clearest illustration Jesus could find of the importance of channeling the impulse of anger into the fruit of repentance.

Kenyan Christians have ample reason to feel anger toward certain Muslims who engage in acts of violence and terror, incidents like the Westgate and Garissa terrorist attacks that shake the country and its people to the core. The fact that some are using the language of Samaritans means that they are locating themselves, whether intentionally or not, in a subversive narrative that draws them to transform that anger.

We all need help transforming our anger. Jesus is not disappointed by it, but loves us so deeply that he offers us a way out of the kind of anger that leads to hatred. Could it be that the Samaritans in our own lives represent the path of deliverance, as they did for the disciples?

Repentance means that we do not read ourselves into Scripture as the heroes, but as witnesses.[19] We are tempted to identify with those who come out in the right, who have seen all along who Jesus was, who were able to look past their own prejudice into the heart of the matter.

If being heroes is our approach to Scripture, we lose the power of the story to bring about transformation in our thinking and behavior. We are forgiven and brought into a story not of our own making. Jesus invites repentance for entanglements like racism, nationalism, and greed.[20]

Central to this call to repentance is the glaring chasm of poverty and wealth. In the age of globalization, the first line of the church's reconciling work is to address the gap between the rich and the poor.[21]

The gift he gives us on this path of deliverance is the Samaritan – the Muslim.

The third test: *Does the label promote mutuality?*

The familiarity of the Good Samaritan parable can obscure the startling fact that when Jesus is most directly asked what undergirds his ethic of neighbor love, he points to a person of a different religion.

Jesus did not hover above religion. He did not appear out of thin air--he was a Palestinian Jew. As much as for his hearers, the Samaritans were the religious other for *Jesus himself*. They were strange, they were misguided, they were sometimes hostile.

And *yet*--he is saying in clear language that his followers should be taught by those of other faiths, that we must learn from their examples as much as we intend to teach them.

If Kenyan Christians have primed themselves to see Somalis as Samaritans, when they are confronted with extraordinary acts of kindness and sacrifice--as in the Mandera bus incident--it connects naturally to the heart of Jesus' intended meaning for the parable. We are meant to be each other's teachers and each other's students.

Just as the Kenyan pastor referred to Somalis as *our Samaritans*, should the rest of us follow this example in seeing Muslims more generally as *our Samaritans*?

It depends. Do we use the word *our* in a possessive, territorial, or defensive sense?

Or do we use it to mean what Jesus intended: to us, Muslims operate as the Samaritans did for Jesus? Our Muslim neighbors help us to turn our scrutiny inwards, to humble ourselves, and to repent from our sins. They become our moral teachers and exemplars. Our feelings of anger may be stirred against them, and we learn from Jesus to transform these sentiments into love.

Name-calling is an important calling if we are serious about our faith! Labels have the power to transform. So it matters that we are steeped in the parables and deeds of Jesus, and that we are asking along with Kenyan evangelicals *how we fit into the stories* – and how those around us do as well.

A significant study of US evangelicals shows that attitudes toward immigrants, including Muslims, are shaped enormously by several factors. First, do we worship and serve alongside immigrants? And second, are we regularly hearing the stories of Scripture, including the parable of the Good Samaritan?[22]

You are what you eat is spiritually true. We become the stories we live into, and they shape us in ways we are not even aware of.

This is the meaning and the power of name-calling. We might think we are telling a Samaritan story. But it's actually telling *us*, turning a mirror onto our weaknesses and making us stronger along with the other.

It also prepares us to be better guests of God--where we now turn our attention.

NOTES

[1] David Bosch, *Transforming Mission: Paradigm Shifts in Theology and Mission*, 20th anniversary ed., (Maryknoll, NY: Orbis, 2011), 93.

[2] David Zarembka, "Game Changer in the War against Terror" African Great Lakes Initiative of Friends Peace Teams, Report from Kenya #368, January 1, 2016. Available at http://aglifpt.org/rfk/?p=735.

[3] Tizon, *Whole and Reconciled*, 63-74.

[4] Volf, *Allah*, 259.

[5] Ibid., 76.

[6] Marc Gopin, *Holy War, Holy Peace: How Religion Can Bring Peace to the Middle East* (New York: Oxford University Press, 2002), 12-15.

[7] Ken Chitwood, "Somalis as Samaritans: A Glimpse into Christian-Muslim Relations in Eastern Africa from the Perspective of Evangelical Kenyan Christians," *Islam and Christian-Muslim Relations*, vol. 28, no. 1 (2017), 77.

[8] Glaser, *Bible and Other Faiths*, 65.

[9] Gopin, *Holy War, Holy Peace*, 58-61.

[10] Several hundred people identifying as Samaritan live in Israel today. It is important to clarify that the symbolic label of Samaritan in the New Testament and its modern applications are not in specific reference to this community.

[11] Newton Kahumbi Maina, cited in Chitwood, "Somalis as Samaritans," 76.

[12] Al Tizon, *Whole and Reconciled: Gospel, Church, and Mission in a Fractured World* (Grand Rapids, MI: Baker Academic, 2018), 24. For a more detailed argument on this see Gregory A. Boyd, *The Myth of a Christian Nation: How the Quest for Political Power Is Destroying the Church* (Grand Rapids, MI: Zondervan, 2005).

[13] Chitwood, "Somalis as Samaritans," 78-79.

[14] Ibid., 83.

[15] UNHCR report, "Somalia Refugee Crisis Explained" (July 17, 2023); available at https://www.unrefugees.org/news/somalia-refugee-crisis-explained/.

[16] Bosch, *Transforming Mission*, 106.

[17] Yong, *Hospitality and the Other*, 103.

[18] Eliza Griswold, *The Tenth Parallel: Dispatches from the Fault Line Between Christianity and Islam* (New York: Farrar, Straus, and Giroux, 2010), 128-130.

[19] Stanley Hauerwas, *A Better Hope: Resources for a Church Confronting Capitalism, Democracy, and Postmodernity* (Grand Rapids, MI: Brazos, 2000), 130. Service workers who approach their ministry with a hero identity discover that moral superiority is incompatible with a mission of Jesus. Michelle Kao Nakphong reflects on her ministry in Thailand: "The people I was trying to show Jesus' love to were better at showing love than I was. How were they to see Jesus and His love for them if I wasn't able to be more loving than they?... I believed that showing a spiritual and moral superiority was the way to minister to people. My stronger character and righteous acts would show people what they were lacking, and at their low point of discouragement, I could introduce Jesus' higher way. It was a self-righteous approach that was actually inconsistent with Jesus' own ministry. On the contrary, Jesus never broadcast nor flaunted His own perfection, but was instead present and accessible to those around Him." Michelle Kao Nakphong, "Bringing a Dish to Share with the World," in Krieg and Singleterry, eds., *Voices Rising*, Kindle edition locations 395-97.

[20] Stassen, *Thicker Jesus*, 16-17.

[21] Tizon, *Whole and Reconciled*, 15.

[22] Ruth M. Melkonian-Hoover and Lyman A. Kellstedt, *Evangelicals and Immigration: Fault Lines Among the Faithful* (New York: Palgrave Macmillan, 2019), 160.

Part III: God's Guests

When I was growing up, we played a sped-up version of Monopoly--dealing the properties, so that you could start earning massive stacks immediately (if the dice fell in your favor). So when I encountered people who actually played by the official rules, I was dumbfounded. It was my first exposure to the idea of *house rules*.

House rules is an important concept in guesting across faiths. In the following chapters we consider *God as our host*. Does God have house rules?

If we want to be good guests of God as Christians and Muslims, sharing the space God has made for us, we need to honor three house rules:

Rule #1: Do not harm a fellow guest. Rule #2: Do not look down on a fellow guest. Rule #3: Appreciate what the Host is doing for you.

Seems basic, right? It is.

And yet it is not. The rules get increasingly more difficult. And unlike our sped-up house rules version of Monopoly, there is no fast-forward button here.

There is no way to jump to the last rule--the most important of them all--without honoring the first two.

God is waiting. God has prepared a table for us. Are we ready to be God's guests?

CHAPTER 8

Mediators

House rule #1: Do not harm a fellow guest.

I was on a bus in Tanzania, catching a ride between cities. The only other foreigner in the vehicle tapped me on the shoulder.

"What are you doing here?" she asked.

"I teach ethics and peacebuilding at a university in Zanzibar."

"That's a Muslim island. Is it a religious program?"

"Yes, we work together as Muslims and Christians. I belong to a Mennonite church."

She asked me about Mennonites. When she heard that it is a pacifist tradition, she exclaimed, "I'm pacifist too!"

Then she paused and reflected a moment. "Well, unless someone attacked my family." After further thought she added, "Or my country."

What else does that leave? I wondered.

My fellow traveler was expressing a common sentiment. We all want to be peacemakers, if we take our faith seriously. We want to own that identity. We hold up peace as an ideal and a worthy goal. Only when peace comes up against the harsh realities of a fallen world do we begin to qualify it, to add exceptions when violence might be necessary.

I have encountered this quandary in every context where I have advocated nonviolence, from the US to Iran to Europe to Africa.

In some cases Christians are thinking through their commitments to peace in the context of relating to Muslim neighbors. Then the challenge of violence takes on a religious dimension. This is how Nigerian Christian ethicist Samuel Waje Kunhiyop, writing in a situation where Muslims and Christians have killed one another, can make the following leap. He first acknowledges that the ethnic and religious conflicts that trouble Africa cannot be solved by violence, and that the church is called to a ministry of healing and reconciliation.[1]

Then he moves to the verse where Jesus asks his disciples to buy a sword so that he can be counted among the lawless (Luke 22:36). Kunhiyop take this verse to mean that self-defense--of one's family or even one's church--against Muslims is justified. He writes, "in Nigeria, where families and churches have been targeted for destruction, *it would be appropriate for a Christian to use a weapon to protect himself and his family*. It is unwise and irrational not to protect one's household if it is being attacked."[2]

In other words, peacemaking and nonviolence are good. But let's not overdo it.

The American on the bus and the Nigerian ethicist have drawn the same conclusion. Peace is a nice ideal. But sometimes the only realistic way to stop a threat is through violence. Given the examples of ethnic and religious violence that we see around us, perhaps it's not surprising that many come to the same conclusion.

It is a mistake to treat nonviolence as a *principle*, or as a *proposition* to accept. This leads most people to pay more attention to the possible *exceptions* than to the force of nonviolence itself. Nonviolence sounds good, sure. But what about *this* situation? Or *this* one? We tend to throw up our hands with the complexity of the issue. It's easier to conclude that it simply does not matter what one believes about violence.

The good news is that there is a better place to begin! We don't have to accept nonviolence on principle alone. In fact, that's not even the best place to start.

When we base our nonviolent commitments on the *kind of kingdom Jesus announced* and the *kind of king he is*, we see how deeply it matters what we think about violence. It becomes clear that nonviolence is essential to Christian mission, particularly among Muslims.

There is a double challenge here. The nonviolent King Jesus is beckoning in at least two different directions. In terms of ideology, he is looking both left and right, inviting us to know and follow his servant leadership.

On the one side, I've met many Christians who are interested in sharing their faith with Muslims. They are willing to *go*, to *live* among Muslims, to *invite* them to know Jesus. Yet they see nonviolence as unrelated to that calling to share the gospel.

On the other side, there are also plenty of Christians who assume that they can hold nonviolent commitments without putting them to the test through mission. They can be perfectly formed pacifists without the messy work of becoming the guests of Muslims.

I admire the people in both of these camps. But they need each other.

Or better said--we all, on the right and on the left, need a Prince-of-Peace-centered gospel. Faithful mission needs both of these ingredients that depend upon each other: an unwavering commitment to nonviolence, and dynamic relationships with Muslim people.

Why mission must be pacifist

During my doctoral studies I attended a church with an elevator (my only mega-church experience so far).

Many good conversations happened on that elevator. One Sunday someone put me on the spot, demanding a literal "elevator speech."

Door closes on first floor: "So what are you studying in seminary?"

"I'm working on peacemaking, especially between Muslims and Christians."

Door opens on second floor: "Peacemaking with Muslims, huh--so how's that working out?"

Just like that, the conversation was over. He walked away having made his point--that the ideal of peacemaking was like shouting in a hurricane, that the two communities were essentially in conflict and wouldn't see any realistic progress until the return of Christ.

My first impulse was to get defensive. You don't say to people in the medical field, "People are still dying, *how's that healing working out?*" Or to teachers, "Look at all the ignorance, *how's that education thing working out?*"

Then I turned more philosophical. Measuring the value of some endeavor based solely on its outcomes is misguided. There are deeper kinds of value--symbolic, personal, or incremental change.

But eventually I realized the real reason I am fascinated by peacemaking. It is because *I don't recognize the gospel without it.* Jesus as Savior makes no sense apart from his work of reconciliation.

Nonviolent commitment is essential for Christians in relating to Muslims. Why? Because enemy love is basic to the good news that we seek to proclaim. The very character of God, and therefore the very nature of what we mean when we say that Jesus is the revelation of God, is at stake.

I'm not interested in becoming a stranger, with all the sacrifice it entails, for the sake of a false gospel.

What is a false gospel? According to Al Tizon, there are at least four: hate, prosperity, comfort, and empire.[3] Each of these false gospels has a kernel of violence at its core, promising peace only up to a point where a line is crossed and violence becomes necessary.

For Christians seeking to witness to Muslims, it is vital to renounce any allegiance to these false gospels. If we are not preaching enemy love, we are preaching another gospel, not the gospel of Jesus Christ. If we are not inviting Muslims to enter the kingdom of God where love has replaced violence, we are not actually inviting them to experience God's salvation. We are instead inviting them to swear allegiance to some other kingdom--whether to the West and its values, to the promises of a prosperity gospel, or some other false or half gospel.

"Because I follow Jesus, I will never kill a Muslim for any reason."

I spoke this line in the course of a presentation in Iran. Moments before, at the opening of the meeting, every person in the room stood as a video played on the big screen. The Iranian national anthem sounded as the glory of the regime was depicted with images of fighter jets, tanks, and other displays of military power. The messaging was everywhere one looked: that the state, the Islamic faith, and the military were unified in a single project.

How did my statement of pacifism sound to the ears of my Shia Muslim colleagues? I was openly, if subtly, expressing my antipathy for this project – and also for that of my own country of origin.

Did it sound naïve? Bizarre?

My profound hope is that something in that statement resonated in the spirit of my hosts--the message that my attachment to the person of Jesus is fundamentally an attachment to every person I encounter, enemy or otherwise.

I also hope that it pulls us all back from the edge of extremism. Extreme rhetoric on each side feeds off the other.[4] If Christians and Muslims can both starve the beast, it will lose its bite.

Muslims are repelled by Christian violence. They need a practical example of a community that has turned its back on empire and its weapons. Are we willing to declare our total rejection of violence, and our total allegiance to a kingdom without coercion?

We might be surprised by the response.

Perhaps the first mistake we make is to imagine that the kingdom of God is something that we can *see*. When asked by the Pharisees when the kingdom of God would come, Jesus replied, "The kingdom of God will not come with observable signs. Nor will people say, 'Look, here it is,' or 'There it is.' For you see, the kingdom of God is *in your midst*" (Luke 17:20-21).

Jesus is not talking here about the kingdom of God ruling only in the hearts of individuals (as important as that is). He uses the plural *you*, meaning that the kingdom is found among you, not in visible structures but in relationships.

Sometimes we use the language of being *in the kingdom* to describe someone who has embraced Christian faith. But a person does not move into the kingdom of God from some other place; it would be better to say: This person's life is characterized by kingdom relationships. Their relation to Jesus, self, and others resembles the right relationships that God intends. Christ's kingdom challenges every form of domination we exercise over others.[5]

The kingdom of God is present in the forgiveness of sins, in the abundance of life, and in unconditional hospitality that is extended not only to kin and to friends but also to enemies. Thus the kingdom of God challenges empire to its core. And not only government structures, but also religiously sacred places and customs, what Mortimer Arias calls the "holiest of holies."[6] It exposes all self-serving ideologies.

The temptations Jesus faced give us a picture of what his kingdom is *not*.[7] First, the *political* temptation is Satan's offer for all of the authority and power over the kingdoms of the world. Second, the *religious* temptation is to demonstrate beyond a shadow of a doubt that he was the Messiah in the very center of religious life. And finally, the *economic* temptation is to win the heart of the crowd in the easiest manner: provide them with bread. The fact that Jesus rejected all three of these shows that his kingdom is utterly removed from dominating, power-over forms. It is radically invitational, completely non-coercive.

Put positively, the upside-down kingdom that Jesus proclaimed is one in which slaves are free and the poor are rich. The kingdom has clear economic implications, as demonstrated through Jesus' teaching, the lives he touches (such as Zacchaeus), and his continuity with Old Testament conceptions of justice.

This is indeed revolutionary. But how we get there matters. And violence has no place in Christ's revolution.

The ultimate proof of the nonviolence of Jesus' kingdom is the cross. The cross breaks the cycle of violence. It ends the need for a scapegoat, someone to absorb the blame for the ills of the world. The cross is God's final yes to humanity. It is God's embrace of the world.[8]

A betrayal of Jesus as profound as the Crusades (literally, violence done under the banner of the cross) is not easily or quickly healed.

The church recovered from Peter's denial of Jesus. He was forgiven and restored.

The church even recovered from the betrayal of Judas. An apostle was selected in his place.

But this coup against the teachings of Christ[9] --the church has never recovered from this. This level of betrayal lasts a thousand years. Muslims have not forgotten the false gospel of the Crusades--and they never will forget until they encounter Christians who say *We will never do something like that again.*

And until they have reason to believe them.

Jesus' rejection of violence is grounded in the value of human life. His special concern for the vulnerable, and his turning the tables on power, is a declaration of an altogether different kind of kingdom.

But this is not the only reason Jesus rejected coercion. He is also a pragmatist when it comes to violence. Military might appears invincible--but in the end it always fails. For all of Jesus' concern for the poor and for justice, he barely gives the Roman Empire the time of day. He is not obsessed or awed by it.

What Jesus seems to think is most important is that his followers learn to love Roman soldiers in practical, concrete, surprising ways. If a soldier makes you carry his pack a mile, go a second mile voluntarily.

Hardly revolutionary if the goal is to confront the violence and injustice of the most powerful military entity on earth.

Jesus recognizes that *any movement based on even the trace amount of violence will eventually crumble.* There is a force more powerful than the fear instilled by a powerful empire--allegiance from the heart. Total buy-in, freely chosen with no ulterior motive, is the mark of an eternal kingdom.[10] Fear is not a step to allegiance--fear is the opposite of allegiance.

In Iran I observed the long-term effects of a revolution grounded in political, social, and religious control. Ordinary Iranians are distressed by the idea that their country is perceived as hostile. Many have positive attitudes toward the West and toward US Americans.[11] They grieve the fact that politics has cut them off from the outside world. But neither do they want another revolution. Revolutions are radical by definition, with unforeseen consequences.

The attempts to control and coerce are everywhere. When I arrived in Iran, one man pulled me aside and told me in a low voice: "I don't know if you have contact with Christians here, but I advise you not to try to meet them. Save that sort of interaction for virtual spaces."

Behind his friendly warning was the reality that the government guards religious activity carefully. There is space for established minority communities--I visited two large Armenian Orthodox cathedrals. They function more as museums than as active churches, but have smaller buildings where Christians gather.

For unofficial religious communities, however, religious freedom is restricted. Two groups in particular are perceived as threatening: Baha'i and evangelical Christians.

Popular protests around the enforced dress in public for women have resulted in many women in urban centers dropping the *hijab*. In restaurants and hotels, signs state that if women are found without a veil in those spaces the business can be issued a fine.

On a Friday evening I asked my hosts over coffee, "So how was the gathering in the mosque?"

"Oh, I went hiking instead."

Don't you pray in the mosque?"

"No, and I don't know anyone who does all that often. It might be 1-2 percent of the men."

I was surprised. My hosts are deeply religious people. But as one of them put it to me, "*The government is killing Islam in Iran.*" At the same time, Shia Islamic identity remains high. Will people find a version of Islam that they can affirm?

With this level of discontent, it is not hard to understand why Iranians are turning to faith in Christ by the thousands, both within Iran and in other contexts.

The lesson is clear: if you want to turn people away from faith, make it coercive. If you want to ensure the collapse of a movement, infuse it with political pressure, entwine it with military power, and prop it up with fear. In the end the only true believers you will attract are those with insincere motives.[12]

On the contrary, if you want a kingdom without end, let it be completely voluntary, built only on the beauty of truth and love. My concern when I visit a place like Iran is that Christians are tempted to grasp at the same strategies for building the kingdom. Any mission endeavor built on a framework of conquest, even if it is only a conquest of numbers or of social hegemony, is fragile. It will eventually collapse. And worse still, it will do lasting damage to the invitation for Muslims to know Christ.

If the church is to be built on the rock, it must be concerned only with obedience to the teachings of Jesus in the Sermon on the Mount.[13] Any other foundation is sand, and will not withstand the storm. It will be worse than if we had built nothing at all. The lasting damage to the witness of the church is beyond measure. Will those who become disenchanted with political, coercive forms of Islam find anything worth embracing?

A friend of mine works with insider movements among Muslims. He told me, "I agree with you that mission is nonviolent. I'm practically a pacifist. But is it important that we say it so explicitly? It might sound strange to Muslims. Maybe instead they will detect our nonviolence just from the way we talk about and model Christ."

I agree that our nonviolent commitments must be evident in the way we interact. There is no substitute for faith expressed in action. But I find it interesting that evangelicals who emphasize proclamation--witness not just in *deed* but also in *word*--would not see how important it is to say what we believe.

The stakes are high--are we inviting Muslims to live in the kingdom of Christ, or are we inviting them to switch from one worldly kingdom to another?

A nonviolent Jesus might sound less strange to Muslims than we expect. And if it *does* sound strange--so much the better. All of us, Christians and Muslims alike, should be strangers to the patterns of this world, the vicious cycles from which God wants to deliver us.

Why pacifism must be missional

I was describing my peacebuilding work at an event in the US. The woman I was conversing with asked me, "Your mission doesn't try to convert people, does it?"

I said, "Of course it does!"

She was surprised. "My church doesn't do that kind of mission."

I understand what she means. To be focused narrowly on religious identity, concerned only with drawing others into your camp, is a distortion of the gospel. The attitude of pride behind the assumption that *my people have arrived* bears no resemblance to discipleship of the Messiah Jesus.

But what I think is missing is the recognition that *we are always influencing those around us.* If we think that we are encountering the other without changing them in some way, and without them changing us, we are deluded.

There is an adage of marketing: "If you're not paying for the product, you *are* the product." Someone is getting something out of what they are offering you for free. We are influenced and used in ways that we cannot see. If we are not paying attention to what we are consuming, we are the ones being consumed by it.[14]

In the same way, if we are not paying attention to *how* we are influencing others, then we are the ones being influenced in ways that we do not realize.

To believe and follow the nonviolent king Jesus is to share him with other people. Keeping Jesus to ourselves is not an option.

So the question becomes not *whether* we are trying to convert others, but convert them *to what*? And how are we looking to be converted ourselves in the encounter?

A couple in a Mennonite church came to me in distress. Their son was joining the U.S. military. "He was raised in the church, and he's not abandoning his faith," they said. "How could he have missed this part of our witness?"

"What did you tell your son?" I asked.

The father said, "I told him that if he kills a non-Christian, he might be sending them to hell."

There are plenty of reasons why killing is wrong--not least that Jesus is a radically different kind of king. His followers absorb, overcome, and transform evil with good, never with violence.

But I sympathize with the anguish of these parents. They are not alone in asking, How can we introduce our children to the beauty of the upside-down kingdom? And how can we ourselves not find our commitment eroding, as we are influenced by the culture around us?

The answer might seem counter-intuitive. *If we want to maintain our Christian pacifist commitments, we must become the guests of our religious rivals.* That means going to places where Muslims are in the majority, where Islamic norms hold sway, where Christian faith is not culturally assumed.

The clarity that comes from such a move is impossible to find in a culturally Christian context. Paradoxically, weakness or vulnerability that is freely chosen is the only way to take control of the way in which you are influencing those around you. To avoid being simply a product, we must take initiative to create new relationships.

The issue is not simply rejecting military service, or articulating nonviolent theology. Christian pacifism is much deeper--a recognition of the very character of God revealed in Jesus. The quality of Jesus' kingship affects all aspects of our lives--what we do with our time, our money, our talents, our power. In all these arenas we must actively resist the influence of other kingdoms. And the means of resistance is *good guestwork*.

The growth of peacebuilding as a field is a welcome development. But I long to see peacebuilders who are deeply grounded in their faith. This includes the basic impulse to share what is beautiful about our faith.

For Christians who understand how integral peace is to the gospel, the issue is urgent. We must send service coworkers to live among Muslim people, or we will lose the precious treasure our nonviolent king has entrusted to us. Nonviolent commitment is untested until it meets a religious rival. As a *principle*, nonviolence is weak; as a *relationship*, it is powerful.

"Are you trying to convert people?" Yes. Influencing others to consider Jesus is not optional--it is essential. And in giving witness we will find ourselves changed as well. The alternative is conversion--by attrition--to another kingdom.

Learning to love our Muslim neighbors is the most important missiological frontier Christians face.[15]

To cross this frontier, we must reject the false gospels of hate, prosperity, comfort, and empire. These are the mission of the evil one, and have nothing to do with King Jesus.

But a more subtle distortion of the gospel exists. These are the *half gospels* that miss the fullness of the kingdom by focusing only on personal salvation or on social liberation.[16] Half gospels resemble the kingdom, but cannot stand on their own.

A radically nonviolent King will heal the wounds of two rifts. First, the chasm between Muslims and Christians, as we clarify that the choice is not between established Christianity and Islam. Rather, the alternative is between the Kingdom of God and the kingdom of this world.

And secondly, the rift between progressive and conservative Christians. Another false choice exists here--either you care about *peace* or you care about *evangelism*. No – the real options are the good news of the Messiah Jesus or the gospel of Mars, the god of war.

Are these two chasms--between Muslims and Christians, and between progressive and conservative Christians--too great for even the Prince of Peace to cross? Not if we acknowledge Jesus' authority as a *mediator*--the one who bridges gaps considered too wide for anyone to heal. Nothing and no one is beyond his reach.

In Matthew 23:15, Jesus tells the teachers of the law, "Woe to you, you hypocrites! You travel over land and sea to win a single convert, and when you have succeeded, you make them twice as much a child of hell as you are."

What exactly is Jesus criticizing here? Is it the traveling? The attempt to convert? The success in creating converts?

The previous verse tells us exactly what he is criticizing: "Woe to you...You shut the door of the kingdom of heaven in people's faces. You yourselves do not enter, nor will you let those enter who are trying to."

The reason I am hopeful in the power of Jesus as a mediator--and in our own attempts to be mediators as we follow him--is that the gospel is really quite simple. Conversion in the New Testament means simply to give one's allegiance to the kingdom of God.[17]

The kingdom of God is objectively beautiful--to Muslims and Christians and others alike. For Christians to renounce the ugly distortions of false or incomplete gospels will have a transformative effect--on our own discipleship, on our children, and on the divisions between Christians.

To be a missionary is to be a pacifist. And to be a pacifist is to be a missionary.

By inviting others into the kingdom of heaven, I am responding to the invitation myself--from the one who is beckoning all of us to become his guests.

NOTES

[1] Samuel Waje Kunhiyop, *African Christian Ethics* (Nairobi: Hippo, 2008), Kindle edition, location 2535.

[2] Ibid., location 2492-2535 (italics mine).

[3] Tizon, *Whole and Reconciled*, 63-74.

[4] Volf, *Allah*, 259.

[5] Hauerwas, *After Christendom*, 131.

[6] Arias, *Announcing the Reign of God*, 47.

[7] Donald B. Kraybill, *The Upside-Down Kingdom* (Scottdale, PA: Herald, 1978), 9.

[8] Volf, *Exclusion and Embrace*, 291-94.

[9] Sanneh, *Whose Religion Is Christianity?*, 120-21.

[10] Gordon D. Nickel, Peaceable Witness Among Muslims (Scottdale, PA: Herald, 1999), 101.

[11] The warm reception I received personally was counterweighed by signs around town reading "Down with USA/Down with Israel – We will never back down." The country is struggling economically with runaway inflation, in part because of US-led sanctions since the US withdrawal in 2018 from the Joint Comprehensive Plan of Action ("the Iran nuclear deal"). Ordinary people pay the price for the conflict, and are not hopeful about the economic future of Iran unless such sanctions are lifted again.

[12] Lamin Sanneh, *Piety and Power: Muslims and Christians in West Africa*, Faith Meets Faith (Maryknoll, NY: Orbis, 1996), 26.

[13] Glen Stassen, *Living the Sermon on the Mount: A Practical Hope for Grace and Deliverance* (San Francisco: Jossey-Bass, 2006), 200.

[14] William Cavanaugh, *Being Consumed: Economics and Christian Desire* (Grand Rapids, MI: W.B. Eerdmans Publishing CO, 2008), 47-58.

[15] Bryant L. Myers, *Engaging Globalization: The Poor, Christian Mission, and Our Hyperconnected World* (Grand Rapids, MI: Baker Academic, 2017), 13.

[16] Tizon, *Whole and Reconciled*, 63-74.

[17] Arias, *Announcing the Reign of God*, 111.

CHAPTER 9

Mutuality

House rule #2: Do not look down on a fellow guest.

A math major friend of mine in college was convinced that he could beat the casino game blackjack. He claimed to have found the formula for winning most bets, given enough time. Equipped with his system, he strode confidently into a casino.

Within half an hour he emerged. "There was a flaw in my system," he admitted. "The house always wins in the end."

He's a smart guy--and wiser when he came out of the casino than when he went in.

Recall the *Worst Field Trip Ever*, when our efforts to foster understanding were met with anger by the imam in Ethiopia. What was going on in his mind? He welcomed me warmly as an individual foreigner. But when I arrived with a group of Ethiopians, his hospitality turned to fury.

The only explanation is that he was experiencing *fear*. Fear stemming from the struggle between Muslims and Christians at the local level, the national stage--even globally.

The power of fear is evident wherever religious communities meet. Fear moves rhetoric to extremes. Fear revises history by downplaying some chapters, while exaggerating others. Fear sets the tone of the dialogue, and determines which voices are heard and which are not.

In short, fear makes us see the world in terms of *teams*. It is based on the feeling of scarcity, as if we are essentially on sides competing--for resources, for power, for ideas that are either *entirely right* or *entirely wrong*.

Much of the relationship between the two largest religious teams in the world, Islam and Christianity, has consisted of attempts to win at the expense of the other. The competition has taken three major forms: winning the race for numbers of adherents, dominating the debate, and maintaining the moral high ground.

Kenyan Mennonite Bishop Philip Okeyo observes how quickly people fall into this team mentality when dialogues are framed as debates. Radical statements that try to win points will lead nowhere. Intolerance can only be confronted with deep listening, sharing tea, and humility.

He says, "I learned something from watching David Shenk. He was confronted at a mosque for not answering questions. Some of the young Muslims thought they won by trashing the Bible. David only responded with humility. We need to speak what God has given us, and let the Spirit do the rest."[1]

Bishop Philip orients us toward our question: Is there an alternative to this powerful habit of choosing sides? To use the phrase of Martin Luther King, Jr., we need *antidotes* for fear, particularly the competitive kind of fear that paralyzes.[2]

It may be important to distinguish between *competition* and *loyalties*. We all have particular loyalties that shape our ethical decisions powerfully. Mine include: to the Anabaptist tradition, to Christian religious practice, to the church, and above all to Jesus Christ, whose disciple I strive to be.

Loyalties are good. They give us the courage to bring our best selves to the other. And if we learn to name them, we can try to bring them in line with the kingdom of God.[3]

But I don't think I'm the only one--religious or non-religious--who is tired of the competitive game.

The fact is, this game can't be won.

Are we wise enough to learn the lesson my friend learned in the casino, to take the off-ramp from a game that no one can win?

Our deliverance from the useless goal of winning requires going back to the vision and ethos of Jesus. It means finding a better way to interact. It means replacing competition with *mutuality*.

So how do we get to mutuality? Three steps: looking *back with hope*, looking *around with joy*, and looking *forward with love*. The past, present, and future of the Muslim-Christian relationship have tremendous promise.

Looking back with hope: Are interfaith relationships improving?

It may sound strange to use the word *hope* with regard to the past. We're more accustomed to hope as a *future*-oriented idea.

But what if one of the keys to shedding our harmful competition today is to notice that we are actually moving in a good direction? Not just as people of different faiths--but also as humans.

For many who read current events, this is a counter-intuitive idea. Isn't there war and violence all over the news? Aren't things just getting worse all the time?

Well, yes--until we take a long view. Not just a hunch or the particular wars that we see on the news--but actually considering rates of violence and war. Psychologist Steven Pinker lays out the data to prove that for all the dangers we face today, the past was far worse.[4] Non-state societies had murder rates much higher than states at their most violent. Legal, humanitarian, and rights revolutions have brought human violence to unprecedented lows.

The argument is not that we are all peaceful individuals now. But something is working. The philosopher Peter Singer says that over the course of history, people have expanded the circle of beings whose interests they value. The value for human life and happiness has gone up. What could explain this growth in empathy?

One possibility is literacy. Reading is a way of putting someone else's thoughts into your head. When you observe the world from another's vantage point, you begin to see them as different but very similar to yourself. Reading other people's words allows you to enter into their pain and joy.[5]

Christian theologian Miroslav Volf describes the Muslim-Christian relationship along these lines as well. There are seven entities in every relationship--you, me, our images of each other, our images of ourselves, and finally God who alone sees us clearly.[6] Are we getting better at recognizing these seven vantage points? We are, every time we interact. Even the painful moments, like the class visit to the mosque in Ethiopia, teach us to step into each others' shoes.

So the evidence suggests that broadly speaking as a species we are getting better at getting along. But what about Muslims and Christians in particular--are these relationships improving as well?

Christians and Muslims are making concerted efforts at peace in new ways all the time. One of the most striking is an open letter from Muslims to Christians called *A Common Word*, written in 2007 and signed by 138 leading Muslim scholars. The only motive, according to the writers, was to build peace at a deeply religious, popular level, not just between governments. The foundational belief was that humans have the same souls everywhere, and are loved by God. The statement rejected the widespread theories that Muslims and Christians are inevitably at war, and that we are powerless against the history of fear and prejudice between us.[7]

Could there be a more hopeful sign that things are moving in the right direction?

Lamin Sanneh agrees that looking back can lower the temperature on fear. Movement and change are a normal part of the Christian movement--beginning in Bethlehem and Jerusalem, to Antioch and Athens, to Egypt and Carthage, to Rome, to the North Atlantic, and finally to the Southern Hemisphere. There is no bygone golden age to try to reclaim. Nor is Christianity like a patchwork with no design--it's more like a colorful fabric with each new thread chosen by the Designer.[8] Each thread strengthens the cloth.

The moral of the story is: *don't let a map scare you*. The geographical advance and retreat of the church is not the full story.

And also--don't let a map give you false confidence, or a sense of triumph. The kingdom of God is not depicted by numbers, by territory, or by demographics. It consists of human relationships. It is a faith in a personal God, not a theory or a system. And the kingdom of God is not going anywhere.

We can look back in hope on the mission movement as well. According to Sanneh, the West must leave behind the Christendom guilt complex related to colonialism. Even in its imperial forms, Christian faith carried within it the seeds of resistance to slavery and colonialism. Thanks to African missionaries like Bishop Ajayi Crowther, Christian faith is thriving globally. Christianity did not find Africa. Africa discovered Christianity.[9]

If there is any lesson we should learn from the history of Christian mission, it is this: *Don't be afraid*. The kingdom of God is too beautiful to be ignored forever, too unique to be replaced by any rival system or ideology.

I work as a part of a team dedicated to Christian-Muslim relations. It can be tempting to describe our work as critical *because the relationship is worse than ever*, and getting steadily harder. From a marketing standpoint, the best strategy is to point out how vital your product is, and how it is getting more indispensable all the time.

But our team exists because each member has had positive, life-giving relationships with Muslims. This is not to downplay the fear that leads to conflict. We rather want to recognize, to paraphrase Pinker, that for all the fear we face today, the fear in the past was far worse. To put it positively, there are more expressions of genuine friendship, love, and kindness between Muslims and Christians than ever before.

Will this eventually put our team out of a job? We can hope so.

But the work of kingdom living continues--eternally.

Looking around with joy: Transforming competition and shame

I was seated at a café in the coastal town of Berbera, Somaliland. A young man approached and asked if he could join me.

"Are you a Christian?" he asked.

I gave my standard reply: "Yes, I'm a Christian who loves Muslims."

"You really should become a Muslim! I used to have doubts like you do."

"Oh?" I decided to let his comment about doubt slide.

"I examined each religion objectively. I considered each one. When I did that, it became obvious that Islam is the true path. You should do the same."

I thanked him for the kind invitation. I didn't tell him what I was thinking, which was-*Your pitch needs some work*.

For one, he expressed no interest in what I think or believe.

Secondly, he assumed that I must be dissatisfied with my faith, simply because he could never imagine being satisfied with a Christian identity.

But most of all, he saw *objectivity* as the goal. And not surprisingly, he landed exactly where he started--in the faith of his birth, family, and nearly everyone he knows, including one hundred percent of the openly expressed religious identity of his home town.

I wondered how this young man went about comparing all the religions of the world, to decide which one to embrace. Did he have a point system? A tournament bracket? In which round did Christianity get knocked out?

If he wanted to make me consider Islam more seriously, he did not accomplish what he hoped. It only raised my defensiveness.

It made me realize how easily we are sucked into the competition. His comments were all it took to provoke me to retort (at least in my mind) that my faith was actually the superior one. Once we are in that mode, kingdom witness is nowhere to be seen.

At the same time, my thanks to him was sincere--I appreciate when Muslims invite me to Islam. What I wish I could have communicated with this man, if we had had the time to go deeper, was that *I think he was right.* I actually agree with him. I suspect that the versions of Christianity that he tested and found inadequate, *are* indeed misguided! I don't blame him for choosing the rational system of Islam over the theological mess that is Christianity stripped of discipleship. Christianity minus the cross--self-sacrificial, vulnerable love--is not worth defending. Palestinian Christian Munther Isaac states, "When our testimony and witness to the world is not cross-centered, we have lost the battle."[10]

What freedom there is in leaving behind the competition in order to seek friendship! And the antidote to the fear of losing is joy. The book of Hebrews actually connects the *cross*--the ultimate symbol of loss--and *joy*: Jesus endured the cross because of the joy awaiting him (12:2).

Joy is the opposite of competition. It is the fuel of Muslim-Christian peacemaking. Times of common celebration and play, where mutual joy is experienced, can rebuild broken relationships after wars and conflicts.

But here's the catch--joy is utterly dependent on human contact. We've been created to love our neighbors and enemies as ourselves. And it is impossible to do this without experiencing the emotions of the other. As humans we are remarkably wired to understand our neighbors' needs before consciously thinking about them. We understand others by subconsciously imitating them--we can actually feel their happiness, pain, surprise, grief, and excitement. This mimicry is the foundation for empathy and compassion.

We tend to think that our brains are like robots, controlling our feelings. Yet we actually *think with our feelings.* Anger, for example, is not an idea – but tense muscles and a quickened heart rate. Joy is not happy thoughts, but a bodily experience--a peaceful relaxation of the muscles, a posture of openness. Bodily actions precede and guide our cognitive thinking.[11]

Joy in ministry does not result from winning the battle over souls, but from sharing the joy that flows from God. It represents the connecting point between God's emotions and ours. Joy is an often neglected stimulus for mission in the Bible--it propels people to action.[12]

When I started to visit the mosque regularly in Zanzibar, it was because I was propelled by joy. I almost felt as if I had no choice--this was where my longing to be close to my Muslim neighbors led me. From this starting point, I experienced the mosque as a place of calm and peace, a refuge from the bustling city streets outside. A place where I felt closer to God in prayer than anywhere else.

It was confusing to me, therefore, when I shared this experience with a mission leader and his response was, "I would advise against going to the mosque. I do not see how you can maintain your joy as a Christian in an Islamic space. It will rob your joy."

But it was joy that took me there in the first place! Can we hold tightly to the gospel as if it is something we risk losing?

Joy is the antidote to demographic fear. What if Muslims outnumber Christians globally by such-and-such a year? What if we lose ground while they gain? The fact is, this is not our concern--it is God's. Our job, our joyful task, is to step out of the competitive mindset and into the joy that radiates from God to the world.

Joy is what neuroscientists call an attachment emotion. In contrast to *shame*, which makes us want to become invisible, joy opens us up to others.[13] Returning to Hebrews 12:2, we see the same contrast: "Because of the *joy* awaiting him, Jesus endured the cross, *disregarding its shame*." Shame is the work of the evil one, the thief of joy.

So much of what drives the competitive rhetoric between Muslims and Christians is shame. Polemic, the practice of winning an argument by tearing down the other, has no place in sharing the gospel. Finding weaknesses and poking at them can feel like a victory. But in the end all it demonstrates is our own insecurities.

We could learn a valuable lesson from the Dick Cavett principle. Cavett was a television host. One evening as he was welcoming his guests, he turned to the audience and said, "Someone on stage has their fly unzipped. We are all going to turn to the wall and zip up our fly." All of the guests turned and followed his instructions, and the one with the potentially shameful problem was protected.[14]

Shame is powerful--and deliverance from it is more powerful still. What if as Christians and Muslims we were dedicated to delivering each other from shame? What would that look like? Would it make a difference in how we talked about each other? Would it change how we referred to each others' scriptures, prophets, and saints? The news and events that we feed on and pay attention to?

Jesus absorbed our shame on the cross--and fought through it to joy. For his followers there can be only one response: to disregard the shame of others, as Jesus has disregarded our own. Otherwise we become like the unforgiving servant, who was forgiven a huge debt only to turn around and demand what his debtor owed him.

Another word for deliverance from shame is *dignity*. Our human experience of self-worth is deeply rooted in our psychological desire to be treated well--our brains tell us that our lives depend on it. As such, our emotional radar is very sensitive to indignities. They flood us with dread and shame.

But the kind of joy that leads us to vulnerability--to opening up ourselves to others--is a powerful antidote to the poison of shame. The desire to reconcile with those who have harmed us is actually deep within us. Honoring dignity is not the same as forgiveness, but it works the same way--it quickly becomes reciprocal.[15]

Another word for deliverance from shame is *rest*. We struggle sometimes to honor the Sabbath in our own lives, even though we know it is an invitation from God for our own good. But what if our calling is not to just give ourselves rest--but also to extend it to others?[16] Our hospitality toward Muslims includes releasing them from the need to defend their dignity--and inviting them into Sabbath rest.

A concrete way to escape from the trap of competition, then, is to honor the dignity of Muslims. Christians in the West have not always been good at recognizing that we share the planet not with inferiors but with equals.[17] To be dismissive of Islam or to attempt to find its weaknesses is to ignore--or even worse, to try to exploit – the pain in the Muslim world. We should always be seeking what we can affirm in the other. This means taking seriously what Muslims say about their own faith.

We arrived in Somaliland on the very day that members of al-Qaeda attacked the office of the French satirical newspaper *Charlie Hebdo*. The murders were in response to the magazine's publication of cartoons of the Prophet Muhammad, including a caricature on its cover.

All over the city of Hargeisa I observed bumper stickers reading, *We love the Prophet more than we love ourselves*. What was the sentiment behind these messages? From the perspective of dignity, what was going on? The message was obvious: *My identity is wrapped up in the Prophet--what I aspire to be as a Muslim is shaped by him. So when you insult him, you insult me and everything I believe in.*[18]

If we as Christians take seriously that on the cross Jesus replaced *shame*--his own and that of his enemies--with *joy*. The vulnerable openness to the other--then trying to exploit weakness or provoke the other has no place in our lives.

But what about our own shame? When the US government began imposing travel bans and deporting people for criticizing its policies, an Iranian friend wrote jokingly to me, "I hope you don't get deported as a Chadian." I responded, "I am so ashamed of US leadership at the moment." To my surprise, he wrote back, "Why are you ashamed? I am living in a country that has a 46-year past of hostility toward the world. Should I feel ashamed of it?"[19]

What my friend was suggesting is that shame, in all its forms, will eventually close us off to the other. Joy is what opens us up and gives life to the relationship. Only joy can transform the competition. And how do we recognize a joyful faith? It's very simple: one that moves toward rather than away from the other.[20]

Sometimes the competition happens around a particular place. Eastleigh, the majority-Somali neighborhood of Nairobi, is the location of frequent exchanges between Muslims and Christians. A Kenyan Mennonite bishop told me, "I stay away from the debates where people are trying to win. I prefer the one-on-one or one-on-two friendly exchanges. To me a debate is not helpful because the agenda is that I win. And the Muslims always think they win."[21]

How could they not? How could anyone not think that their own faith has won the competition? What sort of shame would be required to acknowledge that you are trying to defend an inferior religion?

If Christians think we can shame Muslims into accepting Christ, and vice versa, then we are sorely mistaken. The only path to faith in Christ is joy--joy that God has come near in Jesus, bringing about a whole new creation where all things are reconciled.

Jean-Paul Sartre said, "Once you hear the details of victory, it is hard to distinguish it from a defeat." A victory achieved at the expense of love is not a true success, no matter how we try to frame it.

Jesus gives us the flip side of Sartre's quote: Once you hear the details of a defeat by execution on a cross, you realize exactly what kind of victory it was. "Having disarmed the powers and authorities, he made a public spectacle of them, triumphing over them by the cross" (Col 2:15).

That is to say, the competition is already won. Any attempt on our part to win is therefore to deny the cross. Our job is only this: to respond in joy to the fact that Christ has defeated and publicly shamed the systems of violence and domination.

The young Somali man wanted me to know that he had looked around with competitiveness. Are we tempted to mirror his approach as we look at the world around us? Perhaps we are called to step into another mode, the kind of joy that opens us up to our neighbor and invites them to know Jesus.

Looking forward with love: Inheriting the earth as an alternative to competition

As a young pastor I was assigned to an interim pastorate. On my very first Sunday with the congregation, a combined Sunday school class was announced on a subject called "end times." The goal was to examine biblical prophecy and attempt to apply it to today.

What have I gotten myself into? I thought.

In a Sunday school lesson on Ezekiel 39, the teacher speculated that the war in Syria was the beginning of the massive bloodshed that would usher in the end of days. He read verse 4, "I will give you as food to all kinds of carrion birds and to the wild animals," then looked up and exclaimed, "Isn't it amazing that we get to see this fulfilled in our times?"

Wait a second, I thought. Let's step back and realize that we are talking about God's beloved image-bearers, women, men, and children.

This is where competition takes us: to an imagined future where we can casually, and even hopefully, predict the destruction of our religious rivals.[22]

If the nonviolent kingdom of Jesus had any meaning in the *past*, and means anything *today*, then it is also the same kingdom in the *future*. In other words, if the way we talk about the future--our eschatology--does not match the kingdom that Jesus proclaimed, then it is not Christian eschatology. It belongs to another system.[23]

I propose a simple test of a true kingdom eschatology: *Does it lead us to love our Muslim neighbor?* If our vision of the future leads us to hate the other--and the ultimate sign of hating someone is to think that their destruction would be a good thing--then we need to realign our eschatology with the Servant King.

I don't actually think that a kingdom realignment of eschatology requires first of all figuring out the precise meaning of all the puzzling apocalyptic passages in the Bible, such as Ezekiel 39 or Mark 13.

The place to start is rather in the Beatitudes.

Blessed are the meek, for they shall inherit the earth (Matthew 5:5).[24] This is the most important eschatological statement we have from Jesus. Why? Because the best life we can hope for--the peaceful inheritance of the earth--comes about not by conquering but by gentleness. Was Jesus implying that after they have begun to rule the world, the meek will suddenly turn to violence and intimidation to defend their territory?

Of course not! They will not fear losing their inheritance, because they came by it gently, in a way that can never be revoked. As is always the case in the kingdom of heaven, the means and the ends are connected.

The biblical alternative to competition is *inheriting the earth*, the gentle, nonviolent sharing of space in which peace and justice can thrive. In fact, this was the vision from the beginning, the first calling to Abraham in Genesis 12 does not promise land at all, but a great name and a blessing.[25] In Galatians 3:16, Paul states that Jesus is the only seed of Abraham, and therefore inherits the land the whole earth. The messiah who totally rejected military and political power ends up the ruler of the earth. Jesus' land theology is inclusive and universal. How then could his followers return to a narrow and exclusive reading of the kingdom, its land, its people, and its boundaries?[26]

Paul's next claim is that in Christ all the boundaries we attempt to create are removed: "There is neither Jew nor Gentile, neither slave nor free, nor is there male and female, for you are all one in Christ Jesus. If you belong to Christ, then you are Abraham's seed, and heirs according to the promise" (Gal 3:28-29). To inherit the land from Christ is to share it in radical ways--with people of other faiths and ethnicities, across economic and gender differences.

But where does the *religious other* enter into this vision of inheriting the earth?

Marc Gopin asks: can there be complete religious fulfillment for believers in a world full of people who do not share our faith?[27]

To ask the question more precisely: is our motivation in sharing the gospel to bring about a world where Muslims are no longer present? Or are we driven by a deep joy that Jesus is the Prince of Peace, the hope of the world? The difference between competition and joy becomes clear.[28]

As Christians, our hope rests in the coming kingdom, in which Jesus is recognized as Lord of all creation, the Lamb who alone is able to unlock the meaning of history (Rev 5:9). That future is guaranteed. Our faith is utterly fulfilled in the knowledge that this is what lies ahead.

But why does Revelation insist that it is a *lamb* who opens the scroll? Why does Jesus affirm that the path to the kingdom is only through *meekness*? The reason must be that the *content* of the kingdom and the *way* it comes about are so connected that they can never be separated. The work toward shalom is not something we do because it is popular or bound to succeed. We work for shalom because we have a compelling vision of it--a vision of a Lamb who has conquered the world. Our task is to find the spots in our existence where the old age seems so powerful, but where the new age has begun.[29]

Our eschatology must connect the means and the ends. Our hope lies in the Messiah Jesus, revealed to be so beautiful that all creation, with full acceptance, will turn to him. To prove the ultimate lordship of Jesus we sometimes quote the promise that every knee will bow and every tongue confess that Jesus is Lord. What is the context of this verse? It is the culmination of a hymn about the humility of Jesus, and reads: *Therefore* God exalted him (Phil 2:9). His meekness is the very reason for his exaltation!

The primary ingredient of a Christ-centered eschatology, then, is *patience*. Patience is the intersection of meekness and love.

At one dialogue in Iran, our topic was the Shia and Christian ideas of *intezar*, waiting for the Messiah. An Iranian scholar compared the two faiths. He concluded the Christians have a more *individual* understanding of waiting for the return of Jesus Christ, while Muslims have a *collective* understanding of preparing the world for the return of the twelfth Imam Mahdi and Isa al-Masih (Jesus the Messiah).

Suddenly the conversation turned to the question of our responsibility to prepare society for the Savior. Will the world become so *bad* that only the Messiah can heal it? Or will the world become so *good* that it is ready for his return?

For some Muslims, preparing the world for the Messiah means establishing Islamic rule, including the suppression of other faiths. Many Christians take the same approach, assuming that building the kingdom means establishing a Christian society and culture, and even using government power to support Christianity. This is the approach of Christian nationalism, a mirror image of Islamic nationalism.

I was keenly aware that I was a guest in a society determined to combine religious and state power. And at the same time, a society with a vigorous eschatology, where *intezar* is discussed at academic conferences. I asked the Holy Spirit what I should say when my turn to speak came.

The Spirit led me to Matthew 13, Jesus' teaching on the wheat and the weeds. I described my garden in Chad, and how I don't allow my little son to tend it on his own. In the same way, we are not the master gardeners. Our calling is to wait for the Messiah to tear out the bad plants, as we might accidentally tear out something that God has planted.

God has invited us all to his dwelling for a reason--sometimes apparent only to him. The best we can do is to learn the house rules--the etiquette appropriate to our status as guests--and treat our fellow guests with honor and love.

How do we become good guests of God? By honoring one another, in the past, present, and future.

Imagine being invited to dinner, and then taking the opportunity to complain about what our fellow guests have done to us.

Or looking across the table and saying, "Why are *you* still here? You don't belong here."

Or announcing to the host, "I hope they leave soon, at least before dessert."

What a dishonorable thing to do to our host! If we are guests together as Muslims and Christians, then in the words of Howard Thurman the first thing we must do is to dismantle the status of enemy.[30] To see one another as fellow guests is to transform our thinking and our language--from fear to hope, from competition to joy.

That's the sort of dinner party I want to attend.

NOTES

[1] Bishop Philip Okeyo lived in Eastleigh for twenty years, raising his family and leading the Mennonite church there. Interview by author, Nairobi, Kenya, June 9, 2017.

[2] Fortress,1963.

[3] David P. Gushee and Glen H. Stassen, *Kingdom Ethics, 2nd ed.: Following Jesus in Contemporary Context* (Grand Rapids, MI: W. B. Eerdmans Publishing Co., 2016), 173.

[4] Steven Pinker, *The Better Angels of Our Nature: Why Violence Has Declined* (New York: Viking, 2011), 30. Applying the same idea to parenting, psychologist Julie Lythcott-Haims writes, "The world is much safer than we've been led to believe, and our child needs to learn how to thrive in it rather than be protected from it" (*How to Raise an Adult*, New York: Henry Holt and Company, 2015, 286.)

[5] Pinker, *Better Angels*, 175.

[6] Volf, *Allah*, 206.

[7] HRH Prince Ghazi bin Muhammad of Jordan, "On 'A CommonWord Between Us and You,'" in Volf et al, eds., *Common Word*, 5-16.

[8] Sanneh, *Whose Religion Is Christianity?*, 36-37, 56.

[9] Ibid., 10-11, 74, 93.

[10] Isaac, *The, Other Side of the Wall*, 161.

[11] Rob Moll, *What Your Body Knows About God* (Downers Grove, IL: InterVarsity, 2014), 54-62.

[12] Reisacher, *Joyful Witness,*16-19, 34.

[13] Ibid., 17. Reisacher suggests we open ourselves to what matters to ordinary Muslims by reading novels, watching popular movies, and browsing the daily newspapers of the Muslim world (p. 159).

[14] Patrick R. Keifert, *Welcoming the Stranger: A Public Theology of Worship and Evangelism* (Minneapolis: Augsburg Fortress, 1992), 111.

[15] Donna Hicks, *Dignity* (New Haven: Yale University Press, 2011), 6-8, 190-193.

[16] Glaser, *The Bible and Other Faiths*, 65.

[17] Wilfred Cantwell Smith, *Islam in Modern History* (Princeton: Princeton University Press, 1957), 305. Cited in Armstrong, *Muhammad*, 265.

[18] According to Karen Armstrong, the best place to begin divesting ourselves of prejudice against Muslims is to acknowledge the way the Prophet Muhammad is seen by Muslims--as a peacemaker and reconciler who was fully submitted to God and the exemplary human (*Muhammad*, 266).

[19] Abu Atallah points out that well-educated Iranians, with their pride in the rich history of the Persian Empire behind them, experience shame at the actions of their leaders. Abu Atallah and Kent A. Van Til, *From Cairo to Christ: How One Muslim's Faith Journey Shows the Way for Others* (Downers Grove, IL: InterVarsity, 2017), 91.

[20] Accad, *Sacred Misinterpretation*, 343.

[21] Interview by author, Nairobi, Kenya, June 9, 2017.

[22] Munther Isaac says of prophesy without love: "I am almost certain that most Christians would be severely troubled if they found out there was a 'Muslim theology of Christians' that predicts our fate as Christians! And would be not be even more appalled if Muslims treated us based on what they believe was prophesied about us? It is time that we stop treating our Jewish neighbors based on such standards – for their own sake!" (*Other Side of the Wall*, 127).

[23] Secular versions of eschatology can resemble these religious visions of the future in their declarations of inevitability. For example, a 2009 editorial predicted: "War with Iran is now inevitable. The only question is: Will it happen sooner or later?" (Jeffrey T. Kuhner, "The coming war with Iran," *Washington Times*, October 4, 2009).

[24] Palestinian theologian Mitri Raheb proposes that we read that the meek inherit the *land*, rather than the earth. Jesus says empires come and go, but the powerless remain in the land--and this realization

frees us from the overwhelming power of the empire. Isaac, *Other Side of the Wall*, 67.

[25] Atallah and Van Til, *From Cairo to Christ*, 123. Atallah adds, "accepting the Christian view that believers rather than places are holy may be the only remedy for the conflict over Jerusalem" (122).

[26] Isaac, *Other Side of the Wall*, 91.

[27] Marc Gopin, *Between Eden and Armageddon: The Future of World Religions, Violence, and Peacemaking* (New York: Oxford University Press, 2000), 31.

[28] Mortimer Arias identifies a crisis of motivation for evangelism, which swings from saving souls from hell to psychological salvation to church growth to radical discipleship. The view of the end of human history also swings from doomsday to human liberation in history. He concludes, "Why did I not see it before? Kingdom evangelization may be the answer to our current crisis. The vision of the reign of God can be the motivating force which takes us beyond the paralyzing effect of our contradictory and worn out motivations....Kingdom evangelization, then, cannot but be *Christ-centered evangelization.*" Arias, *Announcing the Reign of God,* xii, xvii.

[29] Walter Brueggemann, *Living Toward a Vision: Biblical Reflections on Shalom* (Philadelphia: United Church Press, 1982), 122, 131.

[30] Thurman, *Jesus and the Disinherited*, 97.

CHAPTER 10

Miracle

House rule #3: Appreciate what the Host is doing for you.

In my Pennsylvania Swiss-German background, you start washing the dishes while you are still chewing.

When Christy married into the family, she occasionally found herself eating at the table alone. Everyone else had cleared their plates and moved onto the next activity. We were sufficiently fueled up.

What is going on here? she wondered.

Then we moved to Djibouti, where we worshiped at the only Protestant church in the country. The French pastoral couple invited us to their apartment for a meal. We arrived on schedule at 7:00 p.m., and proceeded to the first of five courses. These courses were organized like a dance that moved to different areas of the apartment, weaving in and out of rooms and verandas.

We took the final course in the warm night air on the back porch, and as I leaned back in my chair with the last morsel of pungent cheese in my mouth, I glanced at my watch. It read 1:00 a.m.--we had been eating and talking for six hours!

What is going on here? I asked. I had never experienced anything like this in my life. As we walked home in the dark in Djibouti, Christy (who grew up in France) explained to me that for the French, hosting a meal is an art. The more seamlessly you can while away the hours with your guests, the better you have performed your duty as a host.

I learned a lesson that night that would be reinforced in many different places over the following years. Every culture excels at certain aspects of hosting, if only guests can learn to recognize and appreciate it. Yet the further the cultural and religious distance between guest and host, the more obstacles exist to the giving and receiving of hospitality.

But the deeper gift that evening gave me was a picture of God. God is like the host who artfully moves us from room to room, supplying all our needs so skillfully that we usually don't perceive that it is happening.

God is such an excellent host that we barely even notice him.

I sat in my garden in Chad, watering the plants to help them survive the long dry season, and reading the Gospel of Luke in Arabic. At a snail's pace I proceeded line by line. As often happens when we are forced to slow down, I saw something new.

I realized for the first time how much of Jesus' ministry centered on signs and wonders, healings, exorcisms. *Miracles.*

When Jesus was asked whether he was the awaited Messiah by John's disciples, he did not give a yes or no answer. Instead, he pointed to the works that he was doing. If we are to recognize the Messiah today, and the kingdom that he is inaugurating, we miss something major if we don't look for miracles. But what kind of miracles?

Christians everywhere desire to experience the miraculous. In our Chadian church we sing,

Il y a un Nom, ce Nom vient du ciel, ce Nom fait des merveilles,
ce Nom c'est Jesus !
En ce Nom, les aveugles voient, en ce Nom, les lépreux sont purs, en ce Nom les boiteux marchent,
ce Nom c'est Jesus ! [1]

The insistence of the African church on seeing God's kingdom come in concrete ways is one of the gifts of faith that it brings to the world. To read the Gospels and to believe in Jesus the Messiah is to recognize the ongoing work of the Holy Spirit to continue the miraculous work that Jesus began.

The most important task we have as the guests of God on this planet, the pinnacle of the divine house rules, is to honor our host by *recognizing what he is doing*. Our commission as God's guests is to be witnesses to the ends of the earth (Acts 1:8). But witnesses are not just those who proclaim what we believe *about* God. To witness is first of all to observe. But witness goes beyond observation--it takes the passivity of seeing and *turns it active*. There's an intentionality about witness--it's not just information that goes in through our senses. We *bear witness*, meaning we carry it in our bodies, with the express purpose of making it known to others.

So witnessing miracles is important. Nothing new there.

But here's what we cannot afford to miss: *Christian-Muslim reconciliation is a miracle, as much as any other work that Jesus has done.*

Surprised by signs

Before we go further, perhaps we should clarify what we mean by *miracle*.

There is not one word for miracles in the New Testament. There are *four*. Together they give us an idea what we are looking for when we try to acknowledge what God is doing.

Observe the rich variety in these four words:

1) *Ergon* has the idea of *works*. For example, when John the Baptist heard from prison about the deeds (*erga*) of the Messiah, he sent his disciples to ask Jesus if he was the expected one (Matt 11:2-3). Jesus responds with a litany of healings and other miracles, and concludes, "Wisdom is proved right by her deeds (*ergon*)."

2) *Dynamis* puts the emphasis on *power*. It refers to the inherent authority of God, often displayed through the Holy Spirit. For example, Gabriel's promise to Mary is that the Holy Spirit's power will come over her as she gives birth to the Son of God (Luke 1:35). Later, Jesus

predicts that false disciples will appeal to the powerful acts (*dynameis*) they've done in his name (Matt 7:22).

3) *Semeion* refers to *signs*. This is an act that draws attention to a reality more important than the sign itself. Jesus and his followers are accompanied by signs such as casting out demons and speaking with new tongues (Mark 16:17). But for Jesus, the *demand* for a sign shows a frustrating lack of faith (Matt 12:39).

4) *Teras* means *wonder*, and is usually paired with signs. Acts names wonders performed by the Holy Spirit, Jesus, the apostles, and Stephen. Paul and Barnabbas bring the contentious counsel in Jerusalem to silence by describing the wonders (*terata*) God had done among the Gentiles (Acts 15:12).

What are we to make of all these terms? How can we land on a helpful definition, given that no single term can possibly exhaust all of the significance of a miracle?

Our task is not to try to synthesize all these meanings, but to look at how they *intersect* with each other.

Here's what I mean: Miracles occur at the point where our human works (*ergon*) meet God's power (*dynamis*).[2] We can describe as miraculous anything that is both a sign (*semeion*) of the kingdom and a surprise (*teras*).

In other words, a simple biblical definition of a miracle is to be *surprised by something good*. If these two ingredients--a sign of the kingdom and the surprise element--are there, then we are recognizing what our Host is up to.

When we start there, there is a tremendous amount of what happens in Muslim-Christian encounters that fits the definition of a miracle! I would go even further: virtually every encounter I've had with Muslims has left me with a sense that I've witnessed something miraculous.

Why is this? Because the cultural and religious barriers are so great that we are forced to search for signs of the kingdom. Our eyes are straining--and then it hits us hard. When I went to Iran, I felt uncomfortable, out of my element, intimidated by a society entrenched in a political version of Islam. So I simply asked the Lord--*Let me see Jesus here.*

And suddenly Jesus was everywhere, in the mosques, in conversations over coffee, in interactions with students and professors, in paintings, speaking words of life from a plaque on the wall of my host.

I am convinced that bearing witness to Jesus means first of all coming to see the miracles happening all around us, particularly in our encounters with Muslims. Our Host is doing something amazing.

Three miracles from Zanzibar...and a fourth

After our sudden exit from Somaliland, we were asking God where we should go. We visited some friends in Zanzibar, a Muslim-majority island in Tanzania. God led me to knock on the door of the Zanzibar Interfaith Center (ZANZIC), a Lutheran peace initiative. The Lutheran director greeted me, "You're from the tribe of John Paul Lederach? Then we need you!"

The library was stocked with materials from Lederach and other Mennonite peacebuilders. I looked out the window over the old buildings of Stone Town just as the call to prayer echoed around the city from five different minarets, and felt the Spirit saying, "This is where I want you."

For the next five years I joined a team of Muslim, Lutheran, and Mennonite faculty, teaching ethics and peace in the heart of a Muslim city. It took us two years of hard work, capitalizing on every relationship we had, to finally get a university diploma program up and running.

I've come to realize that the hard work is precisely why Zanzibar was the place where I started to witness miracles. Our eyes are opened when our human efforts (*ergon*) meet the power of God (*dynamis*). In the opening session of the very first ethics course, as I looked out at the mix of Muslim and Christian students, I said, *God, this is something you have done.* The simple fact that this group of people were in the same room, studying and seeking peace, was a miracle.

Over the next three years the miracles were many. In an African context, initiatives and institutions can often feel precarious, which is exactly what kept bringing us back to the gratitude and joy that emerges when an encounter happens. The students were not just from different faiths, but also from different political parties, and different regions of the country. Even a simple class discussion had the potential for misunderstanding and opposition, or for a miraculous moment. And because it felt so precarious, we were on the lookout for the miracles.

Allow me to share just three.

A young Anglican woman named Amani shared: "When I first came to Zanzibar as a Christian woman, I was afraid because of what I heard growing up. I heard that if you touch a Qur'an you will have something bad happen to you.

"But then I started the diploma program and we were reading and studying the Qur'an, and nothing bad happened to me. And I heard that if you go into a mosque you can be attacked by demons. But in our classes we visited mosques and churches, and nothing happened. Instead it was beautiful. And I realized there is actually a lot about Islam that is beautiful. My mind has changed, and I feel that Zanzibar is getting better as Muslims and Christians learn to love each other."

Is this a miracle? To have one's heart transformed from fear and prejudice to beauty and love? It has all the elements of a miracle: human and divine, a sign of the kingdom and a surprise.

A second miracle: A Muslim man named Khalid, a politician, names how hard it is for some in his community to accept interfaith activities. Khalid says, "It is difficult for some of the Muslim people in the community to accept the way of thinking that we have at ZANZIC. But from my perspective it is true – which came first, religion or humanity? Humanity came first, we are all humans, and our first task is to get along peacefully with each other. There is some suspicion. But when I came to the program and was studying with and from Christians, no one forced me to become a Christian. So now I can become an advocate for peace in my own Islamic community."

Has Khalid experienced a miracle, becoming an advocate for peace alongside Christians?

Another miracle: A young Lutheran woman named Joy testifies, "When I arrived in Zanzibar from Iringa six years ago, I had very negative feelings toward Muslims. And for two years I would hear people call to me in the streets, *kafir* (unbeliever). It made me feel really bad.

"But when I entered the diploma program, I was sitting beside and studying with Muslims. And I asked myself, How can this be? What good can come of this? But we are now friends and we love each other."

For Joy, the process took time--years of hurt and mistrust had to be undone. But to land in the place where she can say that she loves Muslims--and perhaps even more miraculous, that they are friends--is something only God could do.

I watched these three miracles unfold before my eyes, day after day in the classroom, over meals in our home, and as the students shared life with one another.

During our five years in Zanzibar, we worshiped with a Lutheran congregation and an expatriate house church. There was no Mennonite church on the island.

A fourth miracle: when we returned for a visit four years later, a small Mennonite church had been established there, by Tanzanian Mennonites from the mainland. With joy we joined them for a baptism. The foundation of love and trust between Muslims and Christians makes anything possible.

The Holy Spirit takes one kind of miracle--the transformations in Amani, Khalid, and Joy--and multiplies them. That's another amazing thing about miracles, they spill out in all directions, with fruit that we cannot foresee.

Obstacles to noticing our Host

Why are we often so slow to recognize the work that God is doing in bringing together Muslims and Christians? There are a number of reasons:

A fear of messy boundaries. Sometimes we find it difficult to accept that reconciliation is actually God's doing. The reason is that we are so attached to religious boundaries that we cannot imagine any other way to organize humanity.

But is God as attached to our religious categories as we are?

Christian hope arches toward strangers and enemies becoming friends--from Peter's encounter with Cornelius to Paul's insistence that ethnic reconciliation is essential to the good news.[3] Paul gets very specific in naming not just two ethnic groups but two different *religious* communities--with their own rules and practices-- finding unity in Christ. There is "neither Jew nor Greek" (Gal 3:28)--the "one new humanity" created by combining these two groups is fundamental to God's work in Christ. Christ's peacemaking work destroys the barrier of hostility between the two (Eph 2:14-15), reconciling people *from* the law and *without* the law into a new social reality.

From our vantage point, two thousand years later, we read into these verses a kind of confidence about what it meant to identify with Christ. *But it was not clear at all to the early church.* It wasn't obvious that Christianity was a single religion. If anything, Christianity was at least two different religious groups thrown together by a common faith in the Messiah. Reading Acts 15, a fierce quarrel over circumcision, dispels the idea of a monolithic, established early church.

Who is responsible for all this beautiful chaos, upending identity markers and reorienting people toward the Messiah? None other than the Holy Spirit. Paul concludes the Ephesians passage with this remarkable verse: "And in him you too are being built together to become a dwelling in which God lives by his Spirit" (Eph 2:22).

This verse should cut us cultural Christians to the heart. First of all, we need a constant reminder that *you too*--that is, even we--are brought into this new community. We are not the default, the standard by which everyone else is measured. We are the guests, and it is our Host who is doing the inviting.

And second, we are *being built together*. The peace process begun on the cross is not yet complete. It is underway by the power of the Holy Spirit. God is the one who reconciles, and we are the respondents and the ambassadors of that reconciliation (2 Cor 5:16-21).

In short, *reconciliation is a miracle*--God's action to bring us together. Messy boundaries are not a sign of unfaithfulness--they are part of the package.

What an incentive for mission! The work of the church means that we are always aware of those outside the church, because part of the reason the church exists is to get them involved. We cannot wait until our house is totally in order, until we've solved all our internal problems or reached a certain size, and then do mission. The early church was always relating to those on the edges.[4]

Am I saying that all Muslims and Christians are united in faith in Christ? No.

But if Paul were writing today, could he write to his surprised audience "there is neither Muslim nor Christian"? Absolutely! The shock with which we read this statement is no greater than that of the first century believers reading "there is neither Jew nor Greek," who were convinced that circumcision and other aspects of the law were too great a bridge to cross.

Like my students in Zanzibar, when Muslims and Christians form friendships that challenge their old hostilities, they experience it as a miracle. And thanks to the Apostle Paul, we have the theological language to confirm that this is indeed the work of Christ.

Can we give our Host some credit? He's still doing what he did in the first century, creating one new humanity in Christ Jesus.

Do you want to be healed? This is a second obstacle to witnessing miracles of reconciliation. Do we have the desire to see them happen?

The questions posed by Jesus to Bartimeus the blind man in Mark 10:51 and to the man with the disability in John 5:6 point to the way of healing: *What do you want me to do for you? Do you want to be made well?*[5]

How do we identify what our desire is? It's simple: *what we pay attention to* shows us what we want. We usually interpret Jesus' saying that our hearts follow our treasure as referring to time and money. But attention is our scarcest and most precious resource.[6]

If we desire healing in our relationship with Muslim people, we will pay attention to the relationship. It's not unlike tending a plant. We will look for signs of life, give it sun, water, and protect it from being eaten away or crushed.

And when we pay attention, we see God at work. Even when the divine power mixes with our human efforts to obey, it is no less a miracle. Attention leads to awareness – our felt distance from God is not that he is absent, but that we are not paying attention.

Another way to identify what we truly desire is to observe *who we choose as our neighbors.* Do the people we choose to live next to reflect a vision of the kingdom coming? A Sunday school discussion in an American church focused on how to reach out to neighbors. One man put it bluntly: "What my neighbors really want is for everyone to keep to themselves."

If we live in a place where our neighbors' only concept of what we bring is that we simply let them live their middle-class lives in peace, *maybe we should consider moving somewhere where our gifts are needed.* Not necessarily where we are wanted. Because as guests and strangers we are not always wanted by everyone. But to a place where the need for miracles is obvious – and where our very presence there is surprising, a sign of the kingdom.

Do we want to be healed? There are two clear steps: Pay attention to what God is doing in reconciling Muslims and Christians. And become a surprising neighbor.

Impatience with what is incomplete. The last obstacle I'll mention is impatience. I'm referring to the sense that we shouldn't apply the term miracle to something that is only a partial picture of the kingdom.

For example, many Christians I meet seem most interested in Muslims once they have already embraced faith in Christ. People ask, "Yes, but did the Muslims you're talking about become Christians? Isn't that the whole purpose?"

I share their hope that every Muslim person I interact with finds faith in Christ. There's a kind of fullness in that healing. It's also what I hope for the people who are born into and embrace Christian identity. We are all on the way – none of us is a complete picture of what we will be.

But to assume that miracles must be complete in order to count is to disregard the ongoing work of our Host. All healing is incomplete, until the time when creation is fully renewed. This is why one word for miracle is *sign*. It is an event that points forward to the kingdom in its fullness.

It's also why the Apostle Paul draws a connection between miracles and patience: "The signs of a true apostle were performed among you with utmost patience, with signs and wonders and mighty works" (2 Cor 12:12).

Our ability to recognize what our Host is doing requires some toleration of messy boundaries, just like the early church. It calls for patience, desire, and attention.

But when we take notice, it's always worth it, because transformation happens.

Joyful witness to miracles

The response to miracles is joy. This seems obvious – when you see something surprising, extraordinary, and good, you want to rejoice.

But perhaps less intuitive is the fact that joy also *leads to* miracles. Joy motivates the kind of encounters where God does reconciling work.

And joy gives us eyes to see that reconciliation when it happens, and the insight to give due recognition to our Host.

Would it not be a revolution in mission if *every* Christian--rather than leaving it up to a few "experts"--reached out in joy to Muslims? It may well require going to Muslim societies, to experience the joy of the Muslim world. It may mean connecting with Muslims where we live. But face-to-face encounters in a shared physical space are where miracles take place. There is no formula or method for sharing the gospel with Muslims--joyful witness is spontaneous, not fabricated.[7] You never know when the Host is going to show up.

In what follows, we'll see what happens when people take steps of faith in initiating face-to-face encounters--and when the Host shows up.

The miracle of breaking bread. During the Iranian hostage crisis, Mennonites in Kansas hosted Iranians for a meal at a community center. More than a hundred Iranian guests arrived, but only after they had first sent a representative. Why? To ascertain that the food was not poisoned, and that everyone was going to eat the same food!

After all was ready, Muslims sat on one side and Christians on the other. Then the miracle began to occur. As they shared a meal they shared their lives--their stories, families, human experiences of studying and traveling--and the religious barriers began to fall. By the end of the night, there were plans to help each other with yard sales, transportation, and child care.[8]

The miracle of forgiveness. After the *Worst Field Trip Ever*, the Ethiopian students wrote papers about their personal encounters with Islam. An increasing number of the Anabaptist congregations are located in majority-Muslim areas. One pastor wrote this testimony: "In 1990 my father went to the Orthodox Church to worship, and on his way home Muslim radicals slaughtered him in a harsh manner and merciless way. My father was 73 years old. As a result of this, my relatives developed an antagonistic spirit toward Muslims, and still now

they are waiting for any opportunity to take revenge. It was a big temptation for me; my relatives expected me to stand with them to take
vengeance upon the Muslims. However, I am a pastor who is preaching
the gospel of peace, so how can I do this? ... Unless we forgive, we can't
share the word of God with Muslims."[9]

The miracle of healing. I belong to a network of Christians building
bridges with Muslims. At a gathering of this network in Kenya, a dozen
Somali Muslim guests accepted the invitation to join us from a refugee
camp. Part of an ethnic group of Bantu Somalis, they are historically
marginalized in their society. Bantu Somalis have been subjugated by the
other Somali ethnic groups, and during the ongoing Somali civil conflict many have been killed or forced to flee the country. This is how they
ended up in a Kenyan refugee camp, where the younger members of the
group were born.

The stories they shared with us were heartbreaking. They have no
home to return to, and no established place in Kenyan society. They are
in an in-between space where survival is a struggle.

The gentle leader of the delegation, Dr. Muktar, kept his left hand
mostly hidden under his sleeve. My teammate Andres and I sat with him
as he told us his story. The previous year, a soldier had slammed the butt
of his rifle on Dr. Muktar's hand, breaking bones and causing damage
that will never be repaired. The skin, flesh, and bones are disfigured, and
the hand is unusable.

We sat in silence as he finished his story. Then Andres reached out
and took Dr. Muktar's disfigured hand, very gently, and without saying
a word. He simply held it, and we were all silent for a while. But the message was clear--*your wounds are seen, and understood, and accepted.* You
don't need to put this aside or hide it as if it doesn't belong to you, or
doesn't belong here. This wounded and disfigured hand is a member of
your body--and in a sense it is also our member too. The pain you feel,
we feel it too.

A miracle occurred at that gathering. After the Somali group shared their stories, they experienced a measure of healing. Up to that point they were on their guard, even defensive and combative about logistics like meals and travel. The hurt from every chapter and aspect of their lives was plain to see.

But for them to sit with a group of Christians and receive a listening ear, kindness, and prayer, was a clear message that in this place they are honored members, and that we belong to each other. What was communicated to them was this: the fact that you have been so excluded in other places is all the more reason for extra honor, or at least what looks like extra honor to our un-renewed minds.

Something changed. A spirit of love and joy broke out. At the closing session, the Somalis proudly shared a cultural celebration with us, with joyful dancing and pouring milk on the heads of their leaders. There was a level of connection and sharing that would not have happened if the Christians had not first been willing to sit with the pain.

The miracle of dialogue. Where Christians create space for interacting with Muslims, signs and wonders occur. One such space is the Eastleigh Fellowship Center, a ministry guided by the Kenya Mennonite Church in a Muslim-majority neighborhood of Nairobi.

Pastor Joseph Ngolla engages in interfaith dialogues at EFC. Usually the atmosphere is cordial, but one day one of his conversation partners became so angry that he slapped Joseph hard across the face. Joseph says, "I prayed to God that I would not be angry. And I just continued the discussion. Later the other guys who were there came to me to say that they were sorry, and that they were surprised that I was not fighting. I said to them, 'You don't know how much Christ has forgiven me, and he called us to forgive.' It became clear to me at that point that peace is the best witness. And from that time my relationship changed with those men."[10] Miracles like this happen on the street, in the mosque, and in homes. Out of these interactions Joseph and the local imam have become friends, visiting each other at home and attending funerals together.

In a highly religiously and politically charged context like Eastleigh, interactions can easily spiral into arguments and conflict. But Pastor Joseph uses language that is familiar to Somali Muslims, citing the Qur'an and its references to the *Taurat* (Torah), *Zabur* (Psalms), and *Injil* (Gospel). He mentions Christians who related positively to Muhammad during his lifetime.[11]

When Joseph spoke in this manner in the mosque, nobody shouted or interrupted. The next day's topic was Isa, and afterward a young man approached him. He said, "I think I am the reason you came here. I worship here but I come away from prayers empty." He followed up with Joseph and began visiting him regularly at EFC. Joseph says, "I did not invite him to become a Christian. Making a disciple is later, Christ says come and follow first, like he did for Peter. I gave him a Bible, he came back to talk about what he was reading. He came later, ready to be baptized, but not because I asked him."

Joseph admits that he had to deal with his own fears related to entering the mosque. Once an imam stood up in the mosque and threatened him with death for misleading young Somali men. He later met the same sheikh at a dialogue, and told him that he was helping students to learn about Isa bin Mariam. Much to his surprise, the sheikh responded, "Oh, so that's what you are doing? That's good--all Muslims must know about Isa." Says Joseph, "So he outlined my job description!"

Why go to the mosque? Because Jesus went to Samaria, and gave his disciples authority to do the same--as wise as serpents and as peaceful as doves. Now Joseph takes Christian groups to the mosque, convinced that "when you open up to Muslims, they open up to you."[12]

Miracles happen when Christians go to the mosque, motivated by love and joy.

Conversations about faith happen in English classes at EFC as well. One day the composition assignment was to *write about a day you will never forget.* A 15-year-old Somali girl wrote: "A day I'll never forget is the day I gave my life to Christ. I was told that Christians were pagans, but then I realized how much God loves me. Now my mission is to share Christ with my friends."

Pastor Rebecca Osiro led a Mennonite congregation in Eastleigh over a time when tensions exploded into a series of bombings. Many churches left the neighborhood, but her congregation decided to stay. They shared worship space with the local Somalis, offered language courses, and helped Somalis with immigration issues. Now the children of those immigrants call her Mama Rebecca.

Rebecca reflects on this encounter: "Does it change me? Yes and No. It cannot change my relationship with God, or my belief in Jesus, or fellowship. But *yes*--it strengthens me when I come to Muslims who embrace the Qur'an. A good Muslim will not approve of killing. A Muslim woman asked me to pray for her son in the name of Jesus, that he would repent of killing in the name of jihad. It is encouraging--it helps me see that we are not enemies, we are created by God to help one another."[13]

Transformation happens when the Host shows up. But these encounters are also motivated by joy, reflecting God's joy in all of us.

One effect of any practice is that it becomes more intuitive the more we do it.

The same is true for paying attention to miracles of reconciliation. Once I started labeling a positive interaction between my Muslim and Christian students in Zanzibar as a *miracle*, I began to see them everywhere.

What if our task is to honor our Host by recognizing what he's doing all around us, and right in our midst?

The Chadian churches sing,

There is a Name, this Name comes from heaven, this Name works wonders,

this Name is Jesus!

In this Name, the blind see, in this Name, lepers are clean, in this Name the lame walk,
> *this Name is Jesus!*

What if we added some lines?
There is a Name, this Name comes from heaven, this Name works wonders,
> *this Name is Jesus!*

In this Name, Christians and Muslims share food, forgive one another,
> *Knock on their enemies' doors, bury each other's dead,*
> *Build each others' houses of worship!*

In this Name, Muslims and Christians give each other shelter, see each others' wounds,
> *Call each other Mama!*

NOTES

[1] There is a Name, this Name comes from heaven, this Name works wonders, his Name is Jesus! In his Name, the blind see, in this Name, lepers are clean, in this Name the lame walk, this Name is Jesus!

[2] One mistake we must avoid is sometimes called the "god of the gaps." We explain as much as we can through science or anthropology. If there are any gaps remaining in our understanding, that's where we plug in god. I use a lower case here because this god does not resemble the God who interacts with us in history. Divine and human effort combine in the miraculous.

[3] Katongole and Rice. *Reconciling All Things,* location 1127.

[4] Yoder, *Theology of Mission,* 111.

[5] If we agree with Gustavo Gutiérrez that "The poor, the other, emerges as the revealer of the Wholly Other," then the restoration of our sight – our ability to see the image of God in strangers--begins with a deep recognition of our need to be healed. It starts with a whole-

hearted desire to be delivered into something better. Gustavo Gutiér-rez, *A Theology of Liberation* (Maryknoll, NY: Orbis, 1973), 205.

[6] John Mark Comer, *The Ruthless Elimination of Hurry* (Colorado Springs: Waterbrook, 2019), 54.

[7] Reisacher, *Joyful Witness,* 31, 54, 175.

[8] Eldon Fry, "Pinky" (unpublished essay).

[9] Name withheld. Essay for *Islam and Christianity* Course, Masters in Theological Studies, Meserete Kristos College/EGST, February 2016.

[10] Joseph Ngolla teaches English in Eastleigh and has regular discussions about faith with young Somali men in the neighborhood, including organized gatherings at EFC. He is known in Eastleigh (and therefore will be referenced here) as *Yusuf,* the Islamic version of the name. Interview by author, Nairobi, Kenya, June 10, 2017.

[11] Waraqa ibn Nawfal was a Christian cousin of Muhammad's wife Khadija. Bahira was a Syrian Christian monk who received Muhammad positively. Najashi is an Ethiopian Christian king who gave shelter to early Muslim refugees from Mecca.

[12] Joseph Ngolla, interview by author, Nairobi, Kenya, June 10, 2017.

[13] Rebecca Osiro, interview by author, Nairobi, Kenya, June 11, 2017.

CHAPTER 11

Jesus Needs Muslims Too!

I save for last the greatest miracle of all.

Abdullah is a Chadian Muslim who is committed to Jesus Christ. We read the Bible together in our garden. We pray. We help each other discern God's will.

Abdullah is devoted to Jesus. So why do I call him a Muslim?

Because when he sets foot in a church building, he is immediately a foreigner--in dress, in religious expression, in culture.

When he sets foot in a mosque, he is among people who act and think like him.

And yet, when Jesus called him, he said yes--at great risk. His family resisted his newfound identity in Christ, and he experienced rejection and loss. When we studied together the verse from the Beatitudes-- "rejoice and be glad, for great is your reward"--Abdullah looked up at me and said, "Yes, that's me." Abdullah is a surprising miracle. And not just to me--to Jesus too.

We learn from Jesus, and the history of the Christian movement confirms, that more often than not, real gifts come from what we consider to be the margins. Jesus is always transforming ideas about who is important, who matters, and inviting the least expected to the middle.

We see it all over the life of Jesus. Who does he pay attention to? Whose needs does he respond to, when they call out to him in the street?

Who does he stop his busy schedule for, and face with his loving gaze, inviting his disciples to do the same? The marginalized, by illness, by poverty, even by age. Jesus says; Let the little children come to me. Not just on the outskirts, picking up moral teachings by osmosis. He doesn't just say to parents, *You teach them what you learn from me.* No, he calls them into the center, from the edges. He not only invites them in, but says that our faith needs to be like theirs to enter the kingdom.

Jesus is *not* the center, if by center we mean the worldly perceptions of power, value, and meaning. He is far from these. He was found at the margins, both by birth and by choice.

But Jesus *is* the center, the sign and the power of the new creation. If we belong to him, then where he is becomes our center. Our response can only be an exclusive attachment to his person,[1] with all our other loyalties given lower status.

In fact, attachment--or *allegiance*--might be the best way to render the Greek word that is often translated *faith*. The word is *pistis*, and throughout the New Testament it refers not just to intellectual assent-- the idea of believing something with your head--but to embodied loyalty.

When we use *faith* in a modern Western sense, we struggle mightily to reconcile Jesus and Paul. Jesus taught that salvation depends on good works--while Paul seems to disconnect works from salvation.

But when we recognize that being saved by *pistis alone* actually means that *allegiance alone* is required for salvation, we are freed from the faith-works dichotomy.[2] Then it makes sense that Jesus came preaching the kingdom of God, inviting our participation.[3]

Here's the point: we will be judged only by our union with Christ – *not* according to our intellectual assent.[4] The gospel is the transformative story of how Jesus became king. If Jesus is king, we must move from *faith alone* language to *allegiance alone* language.

What does all this have to do with miracles? Everything.

The greatest miracle we can witness is that those we least expect become united with Christ. Non culturally-Christian people are being united with Christ by allegiance to his kingdom.

This is something only our Host can do!

Jesus did not usually seem surprised by the signs and wonders he was performing. But there were occasions where he expressed amazement – and it was always that he was surprised by *pistis* (or the lack of it).

When Jesus returns to his hometown, he finds that he cannot perform miracles there. He was surprised! Amazed by their lack of allegiance to him (Mark 6:6).

But upon visiting a Roman military officer, he is amazed in the other direction. He exclaims, "I haven't found allegiance like this even in Israel!" (Luke 7:9).

It takes quite a miracle to surprise even Jesus. The only thing that could do it was a total outsider expressing allegiance to him. Can our response be any less, when Muslim people are united with Christ?

One way in which this union with Christ is described is *insider movements*. People from a non-Christian religion attach themselves to Jesus while remaining culturally and relationally part of their original religious community.

What does this look like? To take just one example of many: On the majority-Muslim island of Mindinao, Philippines, a movement of Muslims who follow *Isa al-Masih* is explicitly rejecting Christian practices. Why? Because of their history of subjugation by and hostility against the Christian government. The theological development of this group began with a study of the prophets in the Qur'an, and landed on the conviction that Jesus is central in the prophetic tradition. They made their way to a Christology emerging out of the Islamic narrative itself, rather than a systematic Christian framework imposed from the outside.[5]

Isn't this exactly what we would hope for--people turning to Christ, rather than to the structures of Christendom that have no resemblance to the suffering Messiah?

Often more than others, Muslims who become Christian face the torment of social alienation. The story of Mazhar Mallouhi, a Syrian Muslim who found faith in Christ, is a prime example. Arab Christians urged him to leave his cultural past behind--his name, family religious celebrations, fasting, postures of prayer, the mosque, Islamic greetings and language, friendship with Muslims, and even taboos against eating pork. He became confused and suspicious toward his cultural origins. Only a long journey of rediscovering his roots--and beginning to see himself as culturally Muslim and spiritually a Christ follower--brought him to a point of healing.[6]

How did Mallouhi find Christ in the first place? The answer is surprising.

The miracles that we witnessed at the Zanzibar Interfaith Center show the transformation of attitudes from distrust to love.

But the most important individual in our peacebuilding courses was neither a Muslim nor a Christian, but rather a Hindu: Mahatma Gandhi. His words and actions featured in every course. On a practical level, Gandhi is the best Christian evangelist I've seen.

It turns out that it was Gandhi who brought Mallouhi to allegiance to Christ.

As an Arab Muslim, Mallouhi had a negative view of Christianity from the time he was born. It was the religion of imperial powers. On a military assignment in the Golan Heights of Syria (now occupied by Israel), Mallouhi first began to read about Gandhi's nonviolent movement. What leaped from the page was Gandhi's great respect for Christ. Mallouhi observed that Gandhi took Christian teachings, used them against a so-called Christian nation without Christian principles (England), and won the battle.

Because of Gandhi, Mallouhi's heart was open to consider Christ. He saw an outward Hindu whose heart was transformed into the image of Christ, and whose life portrayed Christ more fully than most Christians ever would. This truth might have been lost on many Christians, but it was obvious to many Hindus and Muslims. An Indian Muslim leader in his address to congress referred to Gandhi as "that Christ-like man," and a Hindu who opposed Christianity in India said, "I never understood the meaning of Christianity until I saw it in Gandhi."[7]

What a remarkable statement! Is it any surprise that Mallouhi, a Muslim who becomes totally devoted to Christ through the example of a Hindu, would reject the necessity of becoming culturally Christian?

There is something profound going on here--and that deeper reality is what we call the kingdom of God.

In the West, the dissatisfaction with current forms of church has led some to the emergent church movement--seeking God at work outside the traditional church[8] Can we extend the same appreciation to insider movements, recognizing that God is doing something new?

Insider movements provoke various responses from cultural Christians. One is outright resistance. Another is assuming that they are simply a transition to traditional Christian expression. But this is not the desired outcome for insiders--to make a radical cultural shift.

A third response--and the one which best honors the Host who has invited us all to the banquet--is to echo Bonhoeffer in acknowledging a simple truth: Wherever Jesus' name is mentioned, it creates space that belongs to the power of Christ.[9]

An uncomfortable fact for traditional Christians is that many insiders refuse to choose between Christian and Muslim identities. They come to accept their new identity without completely giving up the previous one.

Martin Accad provides a helpful image. We tend to see Christianity as just another religious institution, emphasizing form and language, like a building. Then along comes Islam, and also wants to build--on the same plot of land! In this way of thinking, the building of Islam must first be destroyed before we can replace it with the building of Christianity.

But what if we instead saw Christ-followers as a community of the Spirit inaugurated by Jesus, into which Muslims are also invited? The difference from two-buildings thinking is immense: "As a community of the Spirit, we call on the Spirit of Christ to *indwell the building of Islam*, as well as the building of any other religious institution, including Christianity."[10]

When we replace our two-building thinking with Spirit-of-Christ thinking, might it be possible to be a Muslim and a Christ-follower at the same time, as some claim to be?[11]

To understand what I mean, perhaps it is helpful to look at the issue from the perspective of the Muslims I met in Somaliland. For many Somalis, to be Somali is to be Muslim. Recall my experience at the university, when part of the opposition I received from certain students involved the fact that I wrote an article that mentioned Ahmed Haile, a Somali Christian. In the minds of my accusers, what I was arguing was that it was possible to be Muslim (that is, Somali) and Christian at the same time. In their rigid categories, this was not a possibility.

As followers of Jesus, we want to respond: You are free! Christ has freed us to allegiance to him no matter what other labels we carry.

The point is that hybrid religiosity is a good quandary to have. Blurring boundaries by mixing and matching is not the pressing problem among religions; the problem is rather treating others with disrespect, hostility, and violence.[12]

Is our discomfort with blurred religious boundaries coming from Jesus and the New Testament? Or is it coming from too strict an idea of what church looks like? The church is not a static and triumphalistic mini-Christendom. The church is God's re-creative purposes taking shape in a community, representing new life in the Spirit.

At the same time, the church is always only a preliminary community on route to the kingdom of God. Missiologist Andrew Walls points out the tension: God calls us to be salt and light communities, embedded like leaven--but on other hand to be citizens of a coming kingdom. There has never been a society--East or West, ancient or modern--that painlessly absorbed Christ into its system. From the beginning, Christian religious expression has always been some combination of indigenous religious practices and the good news of Jesus. Many Christians remained in synagogues well into the fourth century, as siblings exploring their own place within Judaism. Christianity is one of the paths Judaism took, not a new invention.[13] In this sense, the early Christians were the original insider movement in the New Testament.

How liberating this is, for all of us! We are not the gatekeepers, charged with deciding who is in or out. We are all strangers to the gospel. Christ is like a candle in the middle of the table. The miracle is that as we turn to Christ, in his light we see the faces of others who are also turning to him from different seats at the table.

Lest we forget the warning of our Host, the one who organized the party, about who is first and who is last--the narrow door applies to people who assume they are already on the inside (Luke 13:22-30). But people from far-flung places will enter the kingdom.

If that's not a miracle worth noticing, then nothing is.

NOTES

[1] Dietrich Bonhoeffer, *The Cost of Discipleship*, trans. H.R. Fuller (New York: Touchstone, 1995), 59.

[2] Matthew W. Bates, *Salvation by Allegiance Alone: Rethinking Faith, Works, and the Gospel of Jesus the King* (Grand Rapids, MI: Baker, 2017), 12-13. Bates asserts that *pistis* as allegiance does not violate Paul's idea, as Paul's *pistis*-not-works polemic "seeks to undercut any rule-based system--and the law of Moses is Paul's premier example – that enshrines an alternative system of worth and preempts allegiance to the king" (127).

[3] The Enlightenment and the Protestant Reformation convinced Western people that religion is about believing rather than doing. Protestants think that religion is about making sense of life – while for Muslims, ritual practice is the essence of faith. In fact, there is a deep kinship in our traditions, as the five pillars come from Christian and

Jewish practices. The Reformation erased these similarities with medieval Christianity. Dyrness, *Insider Jesus,* 102-110.

[4] Bates states that the truism that a person must have faith or believe in Jesus to be saved is a "dangerous half-truth. With its anti-evidential, anti-rational, and 'leap' connotations, the English word *faith* is of limited value when discussing eternal salvation in our present cultural climate." Bates, *Salvation by Allegiance Alone,* 212-13.

[5] Dyrness, *Insider Jesus,* 94-95.

[6] Chandler, *Pilgrims,* 105-7.

[7] Ibid, 21. A Hindu intellectual stated that what Christian missionaries had been unable to do in half a century of mission work, Gandhi as a Hindu did by his life and his response to evil, namely "turned the eyes of India toward the cross" (130).

[8] One example of research suggesting a fresh approach to church is David Kinnamon and Gabe Lyons, *unchristian: What a New Generation Really Thinks about Christianity* (Grand Rapids, MI: BakerBooks, 2007), 68-70.

[9] Dyrness, *Insider Jesus,* 133-39.

[10] Accad, *Sacred Misinterpretation,* 21.

[11] David Shenk argues that the category of *hypocrites* makes Christians acting like Muslims offensive to some ("The Muslim Ummah and Global Pluralism," in David W. Shenk and Linford Stutzman, eds, *Practicing Truth: Confident Witness in Our Pluralistic World* (Scottdale, PA: Herald, 1999), 122). But hypocrites would refer to an identity taken on artificially to achieve some goal. Here we are referring to multiple identities emerging from an authentic religious experience.

[12] Volf, *Allah,* 200.

[13] Dyrness, *Insider Jesus,* 125-27, 144-48.

Scripture Index

General Index

Peter M. Sensenig has served with Mennonite service agencies in majority-Muslim East and Central Africa since 2015. Born in Eswatini, he was ordained in Mennonite Church USA in 2008. He holds degrees from Eastern Mennonite University and Palmer Theological Seminary, and a PhD in Theology, Christian ethics concentration from Fuller Theological Seminary.

Peter has done multi-faith peacebuilding work in Chad, Tanzania, and Somaliland. At the Zanzibar Interfaith Center (Tanzania), he and his team developed an interfaith peacebuilding diploma program. Additionally, he has taught and presented in such diverse contexts as Iran, Ethiopia, Denmark, Kenya, Sweden, Oman, Djibouti, Congo-Kinshasa, and the US. His book *Peace Clan: Mennonite Peacemaking in Somalia* describes an Anabaptist missiological approach in an Islamic society. In partnership with the organization Discover Islam, Peter was a writer and host of the *Allies for Peace* film series (2021).

Along with his spouse Christy, Peter is a member of EMM's Christian-Muslim Relations Team. With this team they connect to a broad network of Christians building life-giving relationships with Muslim people in many different parts of the world. They also relate to churches in North America, encouraging Christ-followers in every context to reach out to Muslim neighbors as guests and hosts.